Dazzling
Beaded
Jewelry

diy network

Dazzling Beaded Jewelry

50 Great Projects

Jackie Guerra with Kyle Crowner

LARK BOOKS
A Division of Sterling Publishing Co., Inc.
New York

Series Editor:	Dawn Cusick
Cover Designer:	DIY Network, Stewart Pack
Series Designer:	Thom Gaines
Production:	Charlie Covington
Illustrator:	Charlie Covington
Editorial Assistance:	Michelle Elise, Jane Laferla, Katy Nelson, Rosemary Kast
Technical Assistance:	Terry Taylor, Rain Newcomb

10 9 8 7 6 5 4 3 2 1

First Edition

Published by Lark Books, A Division of
Sterling Publishing Co., Inc.
387 Park Avenue South, New York, N.Y. 10016

Distributed in Canada by Sterling Publishing,
c/o Canadian Manda Group, 165 Dufferin Street
Toronto, Ontario, Canada M6K 3H6

Distributed in the United Kingdom by GMC Distribution Services,
Castle Place, 166 High Street, Lewes, East Sussex, England BN7 1XU

Distributed in Australia by Capricorn Link (Australia) Pty Ltd.,
P.O. Box 704, Windsor, NSW 2756 Australia

If you have questions or comments about this book, please contact:

Lark Books
67 Broadway
Asheville, NC 28801
(828) 253-0467

Manufactured in China

ISBN 13: 978-1-57990-854-6
ISBN 10: 1-57990-854-3

For information about custom editions, special sales, premium and corporate purchases, please contact Sterling Special Sales Department at 800-805-5489 or specialsales@sterlingpub.com.

Contents

Introduction 6

CHAPTER 1
Materials and Techniques 8
Materials 10
Tools 12
Simple Stringing 14
Knitting, Crochet, & Knotting 16
Wire Wrapping 17
Bead Weaving 19

CHAPTER 2
Simple Stringing 22
Brick Wall Bracelet 24
Waterfall Necklace 26
Crystal Anklet 28
Tribal Necklace 30
Candy Cane Lariat 32
Crystal Triple Choker 34
Millefiore Necklace 36
Lacy Seed Bead Lariat 39
Filigree Necklace 42
Leather & Jump Ring Bracelet 44
Shell Bracelet 46
Butterfly Necklace 48
Crystal Watch Band 50

CHAPTER 3
Wire Wrapping 52
Antique Button Earrings 54
Beaded Barrettes 56
Prom Earrings 58
Flower Bobby Pins 60
Stacked Wire Cuff 62
Chandelier Earrings 64

Wire-Wrapped Ring 66
Growing Vine Necklace 68
Charm Bracelet 72
Metal Clay Silver Beads 74
Silver & Crystal Necklace 76
Velvet Pearl Pendant & Layered Necklace 78
Crystal Pearl Bracelet 81
Black & White Necklace 84
Boho Hand Wrap 86

CHAPTER 4
Knitting, Crochet, & Knotting 88
Modern Macramé Necklace 90
Knotted Bohemian Treasure Necklace 92
Bead Goulash Bracelet 94
Knitted Choker 96
Beaded Cabochon 98
Crocheted & Braided Necklace 100
Classic Knotted Necklace 102
Bead Crochet Spiral Bracelet 104

CHAPTER 5
Bead Weaving 106
Fringed Amulet Bag 108
Computer-Designed Flower Cuff 112
Frilly Ring 114
Peyote Snake Ring 118
Loomed Bracelet 122

Contributing Designers 125
Metric Conversion Table 127
Index 128
Acknowledgements 128

One of the questions I'm most often asked is, "How did you get into jewelry making?" The truth is, I scarcely remember a time when I didn't make jewelry! Jewelry making has been such an important and intimate part of my life for as long as I can remember. In elementary school, I made jewelry to dress up my dreary Catholic school uniform. I made jewelry for my friends and family for birthdays and holidays, or just because!

My mother was extremely crafty and a "Do-It-Yourself" kind of woman and my biggest cheerleader. Each time I made something she "oooohed" and "aaaa-hed" enough to encourage me to continue to be creative. She encouraged me to make whatever I was inspired to make. As a kid, I spent summers in Mexico with my family where I would spend hours and hours with my grandmother and aunts going to the *mercados* (open air markets) where artisans from throughout Mexico would sell their handmade jewelry. I couldn't get enough of the long beaded necklaces, the dramatic earrings, and beaded wristbands. When I was in the third grade, my family and I moved to Brazil where I met an amazing woman from Bahia named Aldaiza who taught my mom and me about the physical properties of gemstones and crystals.

As I think back to that time of my life now, I realize how important jewelry making was to me as a kid in building the confidence and creativity I would need as an adult. Each time someone complimented a piece I made I would proudly say, "I made it!" My "Do-It-Yourself" attitude was reinforced, my creativity was stimulated, and my confidence grew. At a time when children are trying to figure out who they are and what makes them special, jewelry making is a perfect expres-

Dazzling
Beaded Jewelry

sion of their individuality and a wonderful way to build confidence.

I feel truly blessed to be the host of *Jewelry Making* on DIY Network. I know what jewelry making has meant to me personally and the opportunity to share my passion for jewelry making with viewers from across the county is an absolute dream come true. One of my favorite things about hosting the show is that I get to meet fabulous jewelry makers who share their incredibly creative designs and unique take on jewelry making. I am inspired by every single one of them. There are so many wonderful jewelry makers who I've met on *Jewelry Making* and far too many techniques to include in one book, so this book focuses on beading.

There is an instant gratification in jewelry making usually reserved for delicious chocolate — but without the calories! There is no right way or wrong way to design jewelry; there is only your way. Once you've mastered some of the basic techniques, let your imagination and individual style take over. Everyone has something beautiful inside and jewelry making is a perfect way to express that unique beauty inside of you. Whether you're a beginner or a pro, remember to have fun!

Jackie Guerra,
Host of DIY's *Jewelry Making*

Dazzling Beaded Jewelry

diy
network

1

Materials and Techniques

Welcome to the addictive world of jewelry making! Whether you're a novice jewelry maker looking for step-by-step tutorials or an experienced jewelry maker hoping to add a new technique to your repertoire, this chapter is a great reference. This chapter opens with a visual tour of beads and findings in all shapes and sizes, then moves on to a review of cool, practical tools. Remember: the more you make jewelry, the more you'll know about the way it's assembled and the fun, creative effects you can achieve. I hope this chapter guides you toward even more fun and creativity in your jewelry making.

A selection of vintage lampwork beads

MATERIALS

One of the most exciting aspects of jewelry making is that you can use almost anything to make a beautiful piece of personal adornment. It does help to be familiar with the traditional materials, though, and these photos and descriptions will give you an overview of what you're likely to use. Think of them as a starting point for your own creativity and imagination, and have fun!

SEED BEADS

Like their name implies, they are tiny and look like seeds. They are made of glass, and can be matte, glossy, or metallic, and in every color imaginable.

CRYSTAL BEADS

These crystals and glass beads are machine-made and are very popular for their consistency of shape and size. They are available in as many shapes, colors, and sizes as gemstones.

LAMPWORK BEADS

Lampwork is a term for hand-made glass beads, usually with more than one color of glass. The artistry of the maker is evident in the colors and precision of application.

SPACER BEADS

These beads are just that: spacers between other elements of a piece of jewelry. Pick the size and shape that best enhances your design!

Swarovski crystals in the bicone-shape and Czech glass beads

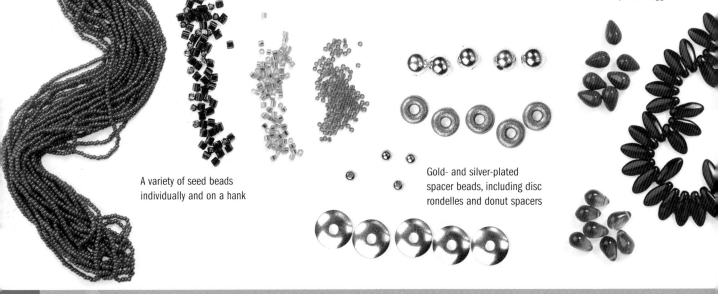

A variety of seed beads individually and on a hank

Gold- and silver-plated spacer beads, including disc rondelles and donut spacers

Drop and dagger beads

DROPS AND DAGGERS

These beads are named for their shapes. Since the holes are off-center, they protrude and provide visual interest in finished jewelry pieces.

VINTAGE BEADS

Vintage beads can be made from glass, Bakelite, marcasite, or various other materials. It's fun to get in touch with the sensibilities of an earlier generation, and it's equally fun to mix old and modern into a new eclectic mix.

OTHER POPULAR BEADS

We're accustomed to precious metals, gemstones, and glass, but don't forget beads made from polymer clay, raffia, wood, and even felt. There are no limits!

WIRE

Nylon-coated wire is easy to work with and a durable foundation for a necklace or bracelet. Wire can be bent and wrapped to surround a bead or stand alone. Beyond the classic silver and gold, there are brass, copper, and even colored varieties.

CORD

In addition to the variety in wires, leather thongs, waxed linen, and silk cord are also used for stringing. The color chosen should complement the design of the jewelry.

FINDINGS

These are the elements that finish off a design and make it functional: clasps, jump rings, and ear wires. Think of them like the buttons and buckles on clothing. You'll pick them to enhance and balance the rest of the design. Sometimes a stunning clasp can become the centerpiece itself.

Assorted vintage beads

An assortment of metal, sandlewood, and quartz beads

Finish your work with jump rings and lobster-claw, hook, or oval filigree clasps.

String your masterpiece on nylon-coated, 28-gauge wire or earring beading wires.

A sampling of leather, waxed linen, and silk stringing materials

TOOLS

With all tools, try to buy the best you can afford. Look for tools that are well machined, sturdy, and smoothly finished. Check for the way they fit in your hands. Talk with the sales staff, who should be able to advise you based on how you plan to use the tools. Look for "jewelers' tools" on the Internet to get an idea of the range of tools and prices. Good tools will serve you and enhance your creativity!

MOST IMPORTANT

Chain-nose pliers

These pliers are a cross between round-nose and flat-nose pliers, with rounded exterior sides. They are flat and pointed where they meet in the center, and are sometimes ridged to help grip.

Crimping pliers

Crimping pliers are a wonderful invention that make the job of closing crimps much more efficient. They have two locations for squeezing: one for establishing a "c" shape in the crimp bead, and the other for turning and squeezing the "c" into a tight, firm crimp.

Flat-nose pliers

The flanges are flat and smooth; they touch each other cleanly.

Check the edges to be sure there are no burrs to mark a soft metal.

Round-nose pliers

The points should be almost sharp points, and the cones should touch each other in the center, like other pliers. They are used to wrap wire and hold the smallest jewelry findings.

Wire cutters

Flushside cutters are flat on the outside and angled on the inside to allow tight, clean cuts. Some cutters are angled on both sides. The strongest are made of titanium. Think about what they will be used for – nylon coated beading wire, fine gold, or thick, hard silver – then choose an appropriate pair.

OTHER TOOLS

Awls and skewers

These tools are used to poke holes into polymer clay beads before they are fired, and also to hold a thread in place while placing a knot. Depending upon use, they are long, sharp and fine, or as rough as a bamboo skewer. The hardware store is a good source – check the nail department.

Beading looms

There are many small looms available for jewelers. They are designed to hold the warp (the lengthwise foundation threads) and allow the weft (the crosswise threads) to be woven in and out with the beads for the pattern.

Beading mat or board

The purpose of a beading mat or tray is to keep the beads from rolling off the table, and to hold them in place as you design your jewelry. They can be as simple as a velour/terry towel from the linen closet, or as preplanned as a molded tray with ruled indentations for necklaces and

WigJig ® Delphi
Patent Pending

bracelets and wells for holding supplies.

Beading needles
It's important that your beading needle be able to go through the hole of the bead and allow the thread to pass through its eye. Other than that, they come in all sizes, and are usually very long and very thin. Lengths of silk sold for knotting often come with the needle attached.

Bent chain-nose pliers
These pliers add a curve downward at the tip of the points, and are helpful for holding an item while staying out of the way.

Burnishing tool
This tool is used for both metals and polymer clay to smooth and shine the surface.

Jeweler's files
These files come in as many configurations as a carpenter's files, but are smaller and finer. They are used to remove unwanted burrs, or add texture to a finished piece.

Jigs
A jig is a piece of plastic, aluminum, or wood with holes in a regular pattern sold with pegs that fit snugly into the holes. Jigs are used to create consistent,

repetitive designs with wire. After the wire is wrapped, it is helpful to temper and harden it with an anvil and hammer.

Nylon jaw pliers
These pliers have smooth, nylon flanges through which wire is pulled to be smoothed and straightened. They can redeem a piece of wire you might otherwise want to throw away.

Pasta machine
A pasta machine (now available in craft stores) is indispensable for preparing polymer clay, from kneading and working it, to blending colors, to rolling out flat sheets of clay.

Jeweler's hammer with steel bench block/ anvil
The hammer is used to temper, or harden, metal and to embellish it. The anvil, or block, should be very hard and very smooth so that it doesn't mark the material being hammered or become dented itself. They come in all sizes.

Ring mandrel
A ring mandrel is a long cone with markings for ring sizes. It's very helpful when the ring needs to be fitted to a specific finger! Bracelet mandrels are also available.

Ruler
A simple 12-inch ruler is very helpful in measuring for a bracelet or necklace. Other measuring tools are gauges that measure the diameter of a stone and tape measures for longer pieces.

Safety glasses
These are essential for any activity where fire is involved, or when cutting a piece of metal that could fly into one's eye.

Tissue blade
This tool is basically a long razor (although not quite as sharp, it should still be handled carefully). It creates a clean cut in polymer clay.

Tweezers
Tweezers come in many shapes and sizes. Sharp points are important. Like pliers, they may be flat, round, or curved. They are used to hold knots in place, pick up stones and crystals, and move beads into place.

Wire brush
This is just like a toothbrush – perhaps a bit larger – and is used like a jeweler's file to remove burrs, carbon, and add texture.

SIMPLE STRINGING

Think back to the first time you discovered beads. Did your eyes roam over a glorious sea of color at the bead shop? Did you long to open that bottle of metallic-blue seed beads, or feel the texture of that luscious carved jade? Did your thoughts overflow with the possibility of limitless patterns? Though the earliest beaded jewelry was most likely made of seeds or berries that had been pierced with a thorn and strung on strips of vines or sinew, the basic technique remains the same — stringing beads. What could be easier?

BEADS

Beads are made from every imaginable material. Bead size, measured in millimeters, refers to the bead's diameter. Figure 1 shows the actual bead sizes in millimeters. The smallest beads are seed beads, which are measured by number—the smaller the number, the bigger the bead. Delicas and bugle beads are types of seed beads. Delicas have squared

Figure 1

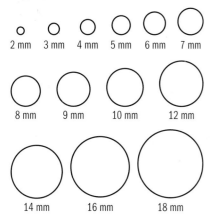

2 mm	3 mm	4 mm	5 mm	6 mm	7 mm

8 mm	9 mm	10 mm	12 mm

14 mm	16 mm	18 mm

edges with larger holes while bugle beads are cylindrical and measured by their length.

THREADS

Some designs will lend themselves to the use of decorative cords, or silk, nylon, or waxed-linen thread. Others will need the strength that tigertail, a flexible steel cable coated with nylon, or flexible beading wire provide for larger, heavier beads. Elastic cording is great for bracelets. It expands as it passes over the knuckles, allowing a snug fit around the wrist. Memory wire, most often used for bracelets, is made to retain its coil — once you've strung the beads, it snaps back into shape. The projects may also call for using wire sold on spools. The thickness of wire is called its gauge. Like seed beads, the higher the gauge number, the thinner the wire.

NEEDLES

If you're using beading wire or heavy synthetic cords, you'll be able to string the beads without using a needle. For all other projects, you'll be using needles that should easily pass through the bead holes. Twisted wire needles, with their big eyes, are easy to thread. You will use them when you're working with larger beads and simple patterns. For beads with smaller holes, such as seed beads, you'll use beading needles. To make it easy, seed bead numbers match needle sizes. However, if your project calls for passing the thread through the beads more than once, you should use a needle that is one size smaller than the size of the beads. Just remember: the larger the number, the smaller the bead or needle.

GLUE

Every time you make a knot, seal it with a small drop of glue. Although fast-drying bead glue or bead cement comes in tubes with pointed applicators, you want to prevent getting glue on nearby beads. The best way to do this is to use a needle, toothpick, or straight pin as your applicator. Put the glue on one of them first, then apply the glue exactly where you want it.

FINDINGS

These manufactured metal pieces are the attachments and fasteners you use when making jewelry. Not only do they close a necklace or bracelet, they can conceal knots, create attachments for multistrands or charms, and hold an earring in place.

Once you have finished stringing your beads, you will need a clasp to open and close the piece. Exceptions are necklaces that are designed to be long enough to slip over your head and bracelets strung on elastic cord or memory wire. There are several options for attaching clasps.

Bead Tips

As shown in Figure 2, position the bead tip with the hook facing out. Pass the needle through the bead tip, then knot the thread. Tuck the knot into the cup

Figure 2

of the bead tip and knot again. Dot the knots with bead glue, and clip the tail close to the knots. Attach the clasp to the hook of the bead tip and close the hook using your chain-nose pliers.

You can also use a clamshell bead tip to totally hide the knots. It closes over the knots, much like a clamshell over a pearl, as shown in Figure 3. Follow the same directions for attaching a regular bead tip. Once the knots are dotted with glue, use your chain-nose pliers to close the clamshell.

Figure 3

Crimp Beads

Since tigertail and flexible beading wires knot so poorly, you will need to use crimp beads for attaching your clasps. These beads resemble small metal sleeves that

Figure 4

wrap around the wire, allowing you to pinch or "crimp" them to stay in place. As shown in Figure 4, when you're finished with your strand, thread on a crimp bead, attach your clasp by making a loop, then thread back through

the crimp bead and a few of the beads. Loop the wire, or knot it if possible, slide the crimp bead close to the clasp, then flatten the bead using your chain-nose pliers.

Jump Rings

You can use these small wire circles to attach a clasp or a charm. With a split on their circumference, they are easy to open and close with one precaution: never pry a jump ring open by spreading the ends apart because it will weaken and distort the metal. Rather, use two pliers to twist the ring open as shown in Figure 5, reversing the motion when closing it. To use a jump ring for attaching a clasp at the end of a strand, loop the thread around the ring as shown in Figure 6.

Figure 5

Figure 6

TIPS | DIY Network Crafts

Easy Threading

If you have trouble threading the needle, cut the thread at an angle, coat it with beeswax, then squeeze the thread flat before trying again.

KNOTTING, KNITTING, & CROCHET

Simple knots and stitches will keep your beads in place while adding decorative touches. (Browse through this chapter for fun examples!) Although the knots are simple to do, resign yourself to at least 15 minutes of practice time until the motions become second nature.

HALF-KNOT

This is where it all begins. A simple half-knot can stand alone, or be the beginning of a half-knot twist. Figures 1 and 2 show the knot being made using four cords. The two inner cords are known as the holding cords, while the two outer cords are known as the knotting cords.

1 Take outer cord B, bring it over the holding cords, then pass it under outer cord A as shown in Figure 1.

Figure 1

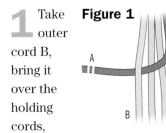

2 Take outer cord A, pass it under the holding cords, then bring it over outer cord B as shown in Figure 2.

Figure 2

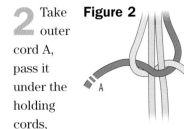

SQUARE KNOT

The square knot is a simple continuation of the half-knot.

1 Follow Steps 1 and 2 for the half-knot.

2 Take outer cord A, pass it under the two holding cords, then bring it over outer cord B as shown in Figure 3.

Figure 3

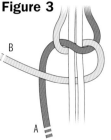

3 Take outer cord B, bring it over the two holding cords, then pass it under outer cord A as shown in Figure 4.

Figure 4

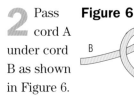

OVERHAND KNOT

1 Make a loop by bringing cord A over cord B as shown in Figure 5.

Figure 5

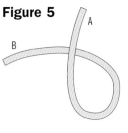

2 Pass cord A under cord B as shown in Figure 6.

Figure 6

3 Bring cord A over the loop as shown in Figure 7.

Figure 7

4 Pull cords A and B to tighten the knot as shown in Figure 8.

Figure 8

LARK'S HEAD

This knot is the perfect anchor when attaching cord to a bead or finding.

1 Fold your cord in half, making a loop.

2 Draw the loop through or around the bead or object you are attaching it to as shown in Figure 9.

Figure 9

3 Taking the two ends of the cord, bring them through the loop as shown in Figure 10.

Figure 10

4 Pull both ends of the cord to tighten the knot around the bead or object.

KNITTING AND CROCHET

Knitting and crocheting with beads involves using wire and thread and the same simple stitches you would normally use. If you aren't comfortable with the basics, find an illustrated knit or crochet book and review the instructions, then find a friend who knits and/or crochets and ask for a lesson. Beads are worked into the stitches one at a time or in groups; just be sure to keep the thread or wire taut as you work.

WIRE WRAPPING

Twist it, bend it, wrap it! Combining wire with beads opens a whole world of design possibilities for making jewelry. Of course you can just string beads on wire— but the real fun comes when you use wire to create interesting shapes in between and around the beads. Wire wrapping is not only fun, it's fast. With only a few simple techniques, you can get started with the projects—you might even plan on wearing one tonight.

WIRE

Where to begin? Copper, brass, base metal, silver, gold, gold-filled, anodized niobium, titanium, aluminum—you'll find a wire for every project. For practice, you might want to buy a spool of the least expensive wire before working gold-filled or silver. When you go to buy wire, be aware of the gauge needed for the project. Keep in mind that the lower the gauge number, the thicker the wire. Each gauge has its own limit—lower gauge wire, with its thicker diameter, is slightly more difficult to work with, while thinner wire may not support heavier beads. Also, different wires have their own "personalities." The more you work with them, the more you'll get to know the right touch needed for each.

You can purchase twisted wire, where two or more strands have been twisted together to create a textural effect, or you can make it yourself. It's easier than you think.

TOOLS

Working with wire means you will need to use cutters for cutting and pliers for twisting and bending. Now's the time to gather your chain-nose, round-nose, and flat-nose pliers. Projects may also call for using a jig, which is essentially a board with pegs that serves as a guide for bending wire into a certain shape. Jigs make it easier to reproduce a shape as many times as you need it, making sure the that the first one you make will look as good as the last.

FINDINGS

By bending the wire, you are able to make the loops you need for attaching your jump rings, clasps, and ear wires. Using head pins and eye pins give you the option of making a dangle or attaching a group of beads. These straight pieces of wire come in a variety of lengths with a stopper on one end—head pins have a flattened stopper, eye pins have a loop. To use them, you simply string on your beads and make a loop. By attaching ear wires to the loops, you can make an almost instant pair of earrings.

MAKING A WIRE LOOP

It's easy to make a wire loop. Once you master this simple technique you can attach a wired string of beads to just about anything you want.

1 Using your chain-nose pliers, bend the wire to a right angle as shown in

Figure 1

Figure 1. If the wire or head pin already has beads on it, be sure to leave enough wire for two or three wraps of wire (see Figure 4).

2 Using your round-nose pliers, grasp the wire near the bend. Using your other hand, wrap the wire around

Figure 2

the top jaw of the pliers, as shown in Figure 2.

3 Remove the round-nose pliers from the loop and reinsert them so the lower jaw is inside the loop as shown in

Figure 3

Figure 3. Then use your other hand to begin wrapping the wire. If you see that the loop is slightly off center, use your pliers to center it over the beads.

4 Using your chain-nose pliers, firmly hold the loop while you use your other hand to wrap the wire around the

Figure 4

neck of the loop as shown in Figure 4. As you wrap, keep the wire at a right angle. Stop when you almost reach the top bead.

5 Use your wire cutters to trim any remaining wire. To prevent snagging, tuck the end against the neck of the wire.

MAKING A BEAD LINK

By stringing a bead or group of beads on a wire, then looping both ends you create a link, as shown in Figure 5. These links are often used in alternating patterns with other bead

Figure 5

links or with twisted wire designs. To make a link, use your round-nose pliers to make a loop at one end of your length of wire, slide on your bead or beads, then use the pliers to make a loop on the other end. Notice how the open ends of the loops are opposite one another. By making your link this way, you ensure a stronger link.

WORKING WITH JIGS

While some projects show you how to make free-form twists and wraps, a jig gives you control when making multiple links of the same pattern. The way you wrap your wire around the pegs in the jig determines the design you will make. You can make your own jigs or buy them. A jig with removable pegs will give you the most versatility — just rearrange the pegs for the pattern you're making. It's always best to use your inexpensive wire to make a few practice designs on the jig before using your "good" wire.

BEAD WEAVING

Don't let the word "weaving" confuse you. The idea of working on an elaborate loom with thousands of threads going every which way is enough to frighten anyone. Just keep in mind that bead weaving is done both off and on a loom.

OFF-LOOM TECHNIQUES

When working off the loom, you'll use a needle and beading thread to string and connect the beads in a variety of patterns.

Flat Peyote Stitch

This is the stitch that's launched a thousand projects. It's simple to master and is the basis for an endless array of designs. All you need is needle, thread, and beads to begin.

1 Thread your needle and string on a bead, leaving a 4-inch tail. Loop around the bead and pass the needle through it again to anchor it.

2 String on seven more beads for a total of eight, then string on one more bead, as shown in Figure 1.

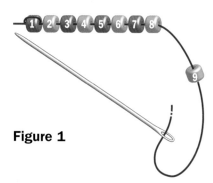

Figure 1

3 Work right to left as you take your thread back through bead #7. String on a bead, and work back through bead #5. Continue picking up a bead and, then entering every other bead until you have worked the row as shown in Figure 2. Then pick up bead #13

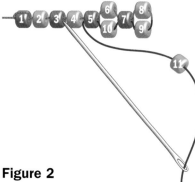

Figure 2

4 Since you want to continue working right to left, turn the work around once you've finished a row. Pass your needle through bead #12 and continue working the row as you did in Step 3.

5 If you're decreasing the beads in a row, exit your last bead and make several loops around the edge thread. Take the needle through bead A then bead B (or through whatever number of beads you're decreasing). Then, pick up a bead and work the stitch to the end.

6 If you're increasing, pick up as many beads as you need for the increase at the end of the row, then string on one more bead. This extra bead becomes the first bead of the next row. Pass the needle through the next-to-the-last-bead, which is one of the beads you added for the increase, and continue working the row as for Step 3.

Tubular Peyote

This technique works the peyote stitch around a tubular core. You will use this technique in the Peyote Snake Ring on page 118 and the Frilly Ring on page 114. By running a single thread and beads back through beads already in place, you are easily able to work in the round. Each row of beads seems to snap into place, creating a tight, brick-like pattern.

1 String your beads and tie them in a circle around the

core or tube, keeping the tail free until later. Figure 3 shows a circle of alternating light and dark beads.

Figure 3

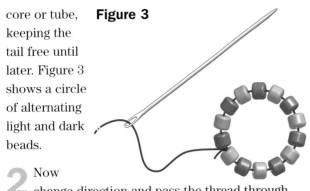

2 Now change direction and pass the thread through the last bead. Add a bead and run the needle through the next-to-the-last bead, then repeat all the way around the circle, as shown in Figure 4. By now you should see that this is just like working the peyote stitch as you did in Step 3 on page 19.

Figure 4

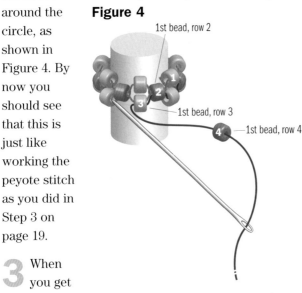

1st bead, row 2
1st bead, row 3
1st bead, row 4

3 When you get to the end of the circle, you will take a step up that will finish the row and bring the thread up one level for starting the next row. To do this, pick up a bead, this is a light bead—then take the needle through bead #1. Now take the needle through the next high bead, slip on a bead and continue working around the circle.

4 When the beading around the tube is complete, tie off the thread. Run both the end and the tail from Step 1 back through several beads before cutting off the excess.

Ndebele (Herringbone) Weave

This ancient African technique creates a strong structure with a zigzag pattern. You'll use a single thread to add beads to an existing row of beads.

Ndebele weaving is used in the Computer-Designed Flower Cuff on page 112.

1 Thread on a stop bead and leave a 6-inch tail. Thread on twice as many beads as called for in the pattern. The number of beads should be divisible by four. For example, for a piece 20 beads wide, thread on 40 beads.

2 As shown in Figure 5, add the first bead of what will become row three. Run the needle through the last bead, skip the next two beads, and run the needle through the fourth bead. Add two beads and run the needle through the fifth bead.

3 Continue to the end of the row: add a bead, skip two beads, run through a bead, add two beads,

Figure 5

Stop bead
1 2 3 4 5 6 7 8 9 10 11 12 13 14 15 16

run through a bead, skip two beads as shown in Figure 6.

Figure 6

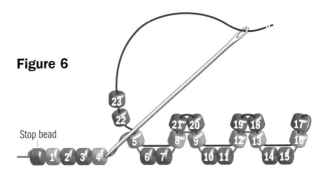

Stop bead
1 2 3 4 5 6 7 8 9 10 11 12 13 14 15 16 17 18 19 20 21 22 23

4 At the end of the row, reverse direction, add a bead, and follow the same pattern of adding and skipping beads. As shown in Figure 7, as you pull the thread firmly, the beads will zigzag into a herringbone pattern. By threading back through the beads of the row below, you reinforce the piece.

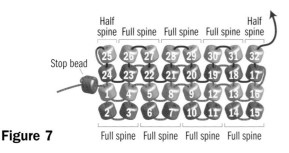

Figure 7

ON-LOOM TECHNIQUES

Loom-worked beads have both a warp and weft much like any woven fabric. The bead loom's purpose is to keep the warp (lengthwise) threads in place as you pass the weft—a needle and thread strung with beads—crosswise around them. You'll use this technique for the Loomed Bracelet on page 122 and the Fringed Amulet Bag on page 108.

1 Thread the loom with the number of foundation (warp) threads called for in the design. They must be long enough to accommodate the finished design.

Figure 8

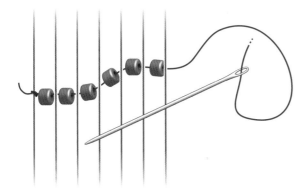

2 Using a single knot and leaving a tail of about 5 inches, attach the weaving (weft) thread to a foundation thread. Thread on enough beads to fit between threads. For example, as shown in Figure 8, if you have seven warp threads, you will string on six beads.

3 Bring the beads under the warp threads to the other side and position the beads between the warp threads. Pull the thread snugly.

4 Using a finger, stabilize and push the beads up. As shown in Figure 9, run the needle up and around the last warp thread and then back through all the bead holes to the starting side. The warp threads are now positioned between the two weft threads, which hold the beads in place. Pull the thread snugly, and push the row of beads into position at the top of the loom.

Figure 9

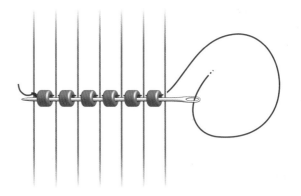

5 Repeat, working from side to side, for as many rows as needed by the design. Tie off the thread at the end and weave the excess thread back through the beads before cutting it off. Repeat at the top with the excess thread left at the beginning.

FRINGE

Making and attaching fringe to bead weaving is an easy way of adding an extra design element. Whether you're making a fun-filled or elegant fringe, the basic technique remains the same. Simply string the beads to the length of fringe you desire. In order to weight the fringe, you may want to string on a larger bead at the bottom, followed by a smaller ending bead.

To attach the fringe, bury a new thread in the already woven beads, exiting where you want the fringe to begin. String on the beads for the fringe, then take the strand up and back through the beads. Follow the project instructions for spacing your fringe, taking your thread through the number of beads given, before making your next fringe.

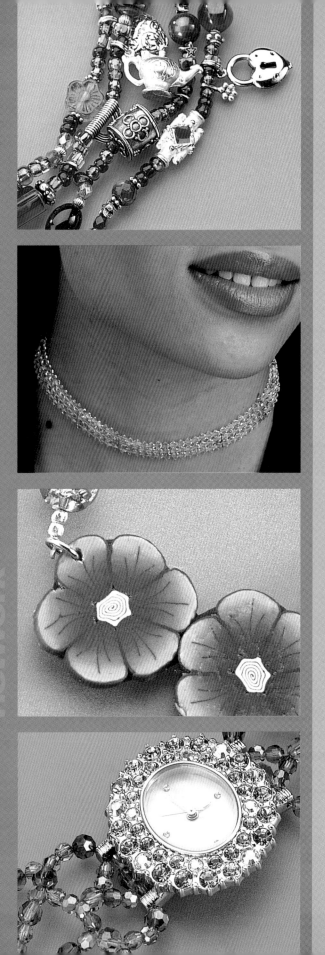

2

Simple Stringing

Remember when you strung macaroni and round candy onto yarn and called it a necklace? Little did you know you were well on your way to real jewelry making by mastering simple stringing techniques. Stringing is probably what comes to mind when most of us think about making jewelry. As adult jewelry makers, you've probably replaced macaroni and candy beads with a variety of beads — from enamel to polymer to shell, just to name a few. You've probably changed stringing materials, too, replacing yarn with beading wire, leather, or silk cord. The techniques are the same, though: just put the strings through the holes. There are no limits!

diy network

◄ Designer: **Steven James** ►

BRICK WALL BRACELET

This bracelet uses rectangular beads to create a brick-wall effect that is sturdy and stunning.

You Will Need

Materials

- 1" segment of sterling silver chain
- 21-strand (.019) nylon-covered beading wire cut into four 10" pieces.
- 8 2x2 sterling silver crimp tubes
- Pillow sterling silver clasp for multiple strands
- 24 2mm Thai silver hex-cut beads
- 48 10x3mm rectangular-cut stone beads
- Tape

Tools

- Wire cutters
- Crimping pliers
- Needle-nose pliers

MAKING THE BRACELET

1 Cut the wire into four 10-inch lengths.

2 Oxidize the silver, if desired, with a commercial oxidizing agent, following all safety instructions from the manufacturer. A natural alternative is to place all of the silver in a sealed plastic bag with a crushed hardboiled egg; leave undisturbed overnight at room temperature, then remove and rinse the silver.

3 Tape off one end of the stringing material. String the beads in the following pattern: three silver hex beads, six rectangular beads, a chain spacer, six rectangular beads, then three more silver hex beads. The chain segment functions as a spacer bar. Place the chain after the sixth stone of each strand, bringing each individual strand through every other link. Once you've completed one strand, tape off the end and proceed to the next strand. (See photo.)

4 Repeat step 3 for all four strands.

5 Test the measurements of the bracelet against your wrist, adjusting the strands by removing or adding beads if necessary.

6 Working on a flat surface, attach the clasp by crimping each strand of the bracelet individually on both ends of the clasp in the same order for each end so the bracelet lies flat.

7 String one crimp tube on the end of the strand. Thread the beading wire through one loop on the clasp and back through the crimp tube. Slide the crimp tube up towards the clasp, leaving a small loop large enough to allow movement of the clasp and crimp. (See page 12 for crimping tips and techniques.)

8 For added security, use a pair of needle-nose pliers to gently squeeze the crimp tube. Repeat the same step on the other side of the clasp and move to the next strand.

TIPS | DIY Network Crafts

A Clean Finish
Be sure to use smaller beads at the ends of the bracelet to create space for the strands to come together where the clasp will be attached. This technique is known as tapering and creates a crisp, finished look.

Designer: **Bethany Barry**

WATERFALL NECKLACE

Create this elegant and graceful necklace by simply stringing beads and making knots. You have the joy of deciding the colors and shapes of the beads, so this project is a great way to use your stash!

MAKING THE NECKLACE

1 Decide how long you want your finished necklace to be and cut four strands of thread 1.75 times this length.

2 Knot all four strands together at one end, leaving a 6- to 8-inch tail. Pin the knot onto the design board.

3 Cut each long end of thread at a sharp angle, seal with anti-raveling glue, and allow it to dry for several minutes while laying out your beads.

You Will Need

Materials

10-20 assorted charms

Assorted beads (6-8mm ovals, squares, teardrops, daggers, and glass donuts were used here)

8 beads with holes large enough to accommodate 4 strands of thread

Center bead

10-20 6mm split jump rings for charms

69-weight upholstery thread

Tools

Split-ring opening tool

Round-nose pliers

Chain-nose pliers

Wire cutters

2 eye pins, 1½ to 2" long

2 Balinese silver cones

Balinese silver clasp

Macramé board or piece of foam core

10-12 T-pins

Nail polish or commercial anti-fray product to prevent unraveling threads

4 The upper side section has only large-holed beads. Decide how much space to put between each bead, and make an overhand knot with all four strands. If there are 7 inches from the clasp to the fourth bead down, make a knot approximately 1 inch down, thread one bead, and make a knot on the other side of the bead. Repeat the sequence of space, knot, bead, knot until all four large beads are in position.

5 The next section, in the front, has beads on all four strands. The top strand will be about 9 inches long. Begin with a group of odd-numbered 8/0 or 6/0 seed beads, and alternate with small accent beads, such as Balinese silver, seed beads, and larger beads. String about 4½ inches of beads and make the next 4½ inches a mirror image of the first half. Place a piece of tape on the thread to keep the beads from falling off and pin this strand to one side.

6 In every location where there will be a charm, thread on a split jump ring between two larger beads to hold the charm's position. If the thread begins to split or fray, cut off a bit, and add some fray prevention liquid. Continue working after the liquid dries.

7 Repeat this process with each of the four remaining strands, making each one a little longer than the one before, and allowing room for the charms to freely hang. For each strand, try to have each half mirror the other half from the big knot to the center and back up.

8 Using the split ring opening tool, install the charms on the split jump rings that are waiting for them.

9 Gather together the four strands and check to be sure the design is pleasing and lays well. Knot all four strands together and repeat the pattern from the other side with large beads, spaces, and knots. (See photo A.)

10 Run all four strands through the eye of the eyepin and make an overhand knot. Make a second knot just below it, then seal the knots with nail polish. Trim, leaving a small tail, and allow to dry. Repeat on the other side, first untying the original knot you made.

11 Run the eyepin with the knotted thread up through one cone, pulling it snugly so the ends are hidden and taut. Make a loop with your round-nosed pliers, run it through the split jump ring of the clasp, and wrap the tail around the stem below the loop. Trim off any excess wire. Repeat for the other cone. (See photo B.)

12 Add the clasp, and the necklace is complete!

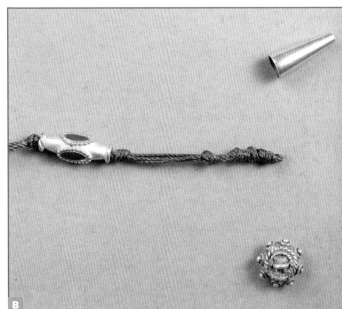

Designer: **Gail Ann Krieger**

CRYSTAL ANKLET

Learn to string and crimp and beautify yourself! Start with an anklet, then add earrings, a bracelet, and a necklace, all with the same techniques.

You Will Need

Materials

15" nylon-covered stainless steel beading wire (0.31mm strength/7 strand)

46 ruby faceted rondelle beads (4mm)

30 champagne colored, faceted zircon, Israeli cut (2-4mm) beads

6 red zircon fancy-cut faceted beads

1 sterling silver toggle (small to medium size)

2 silver crimp beads

Tools

Crimping pliers

Flat-nose pliers

Wire cutters

MAKING THE ANKLET

1 Attach half of the silver toggle to one end of your 15-inch stringing wire with a secure and tight double knot.

2 String a crimp bead, pulling tightly over the knot to cover it, and crimp.

3 Beginning with the champagne zircon bead, alternate pairs of the ruby and champagne zircon beads for a total of ten pieces.

4 String the larger faceted red zircon fancy-cut bead.

5 String 12 ruby beads.

6 Repeat step 3, this time beginning with the ruby pair.

7 Repeat step 4, then string ten champagne zircon beads.

8 Repeat steps 3, 4, and 5 again.

9 Finally, string the other crimp bead and then the other end of the toggle clasp. Pull up any slack in the anklet beads and tie a tight double knot.

10 Repeat steps 3, 4, 5, and 6 again. Next, feed the loose end of the wire through the crimp bead. Pull the crimp bead over the knot and crimp. Closely trim the loose wire end.

EARRINGS

MAKING THE EARRINGS

1 Cut the wire into two 4-inch lengths.

2 Bead the wire in this order: one liquid silver tube, one ruby, two champagne zircon, two rubies, two champagne zircon, one ruby, and one liquid silver tube.

3 Run the strung beads through a crimp bead, then through the end of the earring loop.

4 Run both ends back through a crimp bead.

5 Tightly pull any slack from the beaded wire. Be sure the loop will hang loosely from the ear wire, and crimp the bead.

6 Use the wire cutters to trim the excess wire.

You Will Need

Materials:

Nylon-covered stainless steel beading wire (0.31mm strength/7 strand)

4 pieces (0.5 oz.) liquid sterling silver tube, approximately 1x4mm

2 silver crimp beads

2 earring wires with end loop

8 ruby faceted rondelle beads (4mm)

8 champagne colored faceted beads (2-4mm)

Designer: **Chris Franchetti**

TRIBAL NECKLACE

Natural materials of bone, wood, leather, and wire combine to make this handsome piece. Feel free to use slightly different materials if you prefer a more delicate look.

You Will Need

Materials

- Pair of coil end connectors for doubled 2mm leather cord, in silver tone
- 40" length of 2mm-diameter leather cord, cut in half
- Lanyard hook clasp in silver tone
- 3 feet of 18-gauge nickel silver wire
- Carved bone hook pendant
- 12 painted bone tube beads with at least 2mm drill holes
- 12 latticework wood beads with at least 2mm drill holes

Tools

- Smooth chain-nose pliers
- Strong glue
- Paper towels
- Safety glasses
- Round-nose pliers
- Wire cutters
- Chasing hammer
- Small bench block or anvil

STARTING THE NECKLACE

1 Attach the first coil end connector to the ends of the leather cords. Using chain-nose pliers, slightly flatten one end of both cords, then apply a small drop of glue to each flattened end.

2 Insert the two cord ends into a coil end connector, and gently crimp the first coil of the connector with the chain-nose pliers. With paper towels, quickly wipe any excess glue.

CREATE THE FIGURE-EIGHT WIRE SPACERS

1 Put the safety glasses on. Cut the wire into 26 1-inch lengths.

2 Using the round-nose pliers and wire cutters, make 26 wire figure-eights, with each loop large enough for one leather cord to slide through.

3 Using the chasing hammer and bench block, carefully hammer each spacer to flatten the ends of the figure-eight. (See photo A.)

4 Use your fingers and the chain-nose pliers to close the loops of the figure-eights.

CREATE THE PENDANT BAIL

1 Slightly flatten one end of the remaining wire, using hammer and bench block.

2 Using round-nose pliers, curl a loop into the flattened end and then make a hook curve.

3 Slide the pendant onto the wire, into the curve.

4 Use round-nose pliers and wire cutters to create a backward loop to complete the hook bail.

ASSEMBLING THE NECKLACE

1 String the beads and spacers alternatively along the cords. The spacers are strung onto both cords; the beads are strung on one cord and alternate cords along the strand. After stringing half of

your spacers and beads, string two spacers instead of one. (See photo B.)

2 String the pendant by the backward loop on its bail. Add two more spacers, and continue stringing your beads and spacers to complete the design.

3 To finish the necklace, cut the excess off the ends of leather cording and repeat steps 1 and 2 above to secure them into the second coil end. String the lanyard hook onto one of the coil connectors.

◢ Designer: **Nancy Kugel** ◣

CANDY CANE LARIAT

The impact of this lariat comes from the stunning focal "poppy" bead. When making your lariat, be sure to choose one of your favorite colors for the focal bead.

You Will Need

Materials

Half a hank of white 11/0 Czech seed beads (A)

Half a hank of red 11/0 Czech seed beads (B)

21 Siam Austrian 4mm crystal bicones (C)

14 Austrian clear crystal AB 4mm bicones (D)

4 orange-red Austrian crystal large briolettes (E)

Iris lampwork focal bead

Nylon-coated beading wire (.010)

5 sterling silver crimps beads

Tools

Flexible wire cutters

Crimping pliers

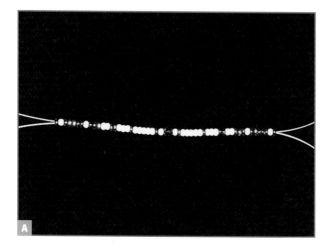

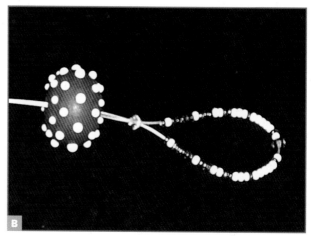

MAKING THE LARIAT

Note: There are four basic sequences used in this pattern. Each letter corresponds to a color/type of bead, as identified on the materials list.

1 Cut two 70-inch lengths from the nylon-coated wire.

2 To start, form the beaded loop by stringing Sequence 1 onto both strands together. Center the beads in the middle of the strands and bring all four ends together. (See photo A.)

3 Get all four strands even and run them through one D crystal and a crimp. Cinch them all up, making sure everything is still centered, and fold the crimp tube with your crimping pliers.

4 Take all four strands again and string them through the lampwork focal bead and one D crystal. The lampwork bead should fit over and conceal your folded crimp. Cinch all the beads together and clip (not crimp) them firmly before you move to the next step. (See photo B.)

5 Release one strand from the clip and begin stringing beads as follows:
Sequence 2, Crystal C, Sequence 3, Crystal D, Sequence 2, Crystal C, Sequence 3, Crystal D, Sequence 2, Crystal C, Sequence 3, Crystal D, Sequence 2, and Sequence 4.

6 Cinch all the beads together and run the end of the wire back through the crimp. Fold the crimp with your crimping pliers, and then trim the wire.

7 Repeat step four on the remaining three strands, using the previous strand as a guide as you work.

BEADING SEQUENCES

Sequence 1 (the beaded loop):

1-B, 1-A, 11-B, 1-A, 3-B, 2-A, 2-B, 3-A, 1-B, 1-A, 1-C, 1-A, 1-B, 3-A, 2-B, 2-A, 3-B, 1-A, 11-B, 1-A, 1-B

Sequence 2:

1-B, 1-A, 2½"-B, 1-A, 3-B, 2-A, 2-B, 3-A, 1-B, 11-A, 1-B, 1-A

Sequence 3
(simply a reverse of Sequence 1):

1-B, 1-A, 11-B, 1-A, 3-B, 2-A, 2-B, 3-A, 1-B, 1-A, 1-C, 1-A, 1-B, 3-A, 2-B, 2-A, 3-B, 1-A, 11-B, 1-A, 1-B

Sequence 4
(used to finish the strands):

1-C, 1-A, 1-B, 3-A, 1-B, 1-A, 1-C, 1-A, 1-B, 1-A, CRIMP, 6-A, 1-B, 1-A, 1-E, 1-A, 1-B, 6-A

◀ Designer: **Jeannine Denholm** ▶

CRYSTAL TRIPLE CHOKER

Jewelry doesn't have to be complicated to be beautiful! All you need for this project are crystal beads and simple findings.

You Will Need

Materials

2 gross 4mm Swarovski clear crystal beads

3 silk thread packs, size 5*

Crimps to close

6 knot covers

1 3-strand sterling silver box clasp

8 3-strand sterling silver bar separators

*For added strength, the silk thread can be replaced with nylon-coated beading wire and sterling silver.

Tools

Glue

Awl

Round-nose pliers

Flat-nose pliers

Wire cutters

⫸ MAKING THE CHOKER ⫷

1 Measure to determine the length of the choker and divide by nine. This measurement will be the approximate length of each section of the choker.

2 String the thread through the knot cover, make a knot, and pull it tight. Trim excess, add a drop of glue, and squeeze the cover closed.

3 Repeat step 2 for all three threads.

4 Thread ten crystals on each thread.

5 Thread a separator bar on each thread. Each thread should be approximately one-ninth of the total length of the necklace. (See photo A.)

6 Repeat step 5 seven times, checking the length to be sure you're happy with the length.

7 Thread the knot cover on each thread, as in step 2, and attach to the clasp. (See photo B.)

MATCHING EARRINGS

MAKING THE EARRINGS

1 Place the large crystal on the headpin.

2 With the wire cutter, clip about ¼ inch above the bead. (See photo C.)

3 Create a loop on the headpin.

4 Cut off the head of a second headpin, wrap a loop, and attach it to the loop with the larger crystal.

5 Thread a small crystal and clip about ¼ inch above the crystal.

6 Wrap a second loop and attach both crystals to the ear wire.

7 Repeat for the second earring.

◀ Designer: **Christine Brashers** ▶

MILLEFIORE NECKLACE

It's so easy to make flower canes with graduated colors of polymer clay, and the result is stunningly beautiful and fun to wear. Make earrings and a bracelet to match!

You Will Need

Materials

2 half blocks of polymer clay, each a different color

Half block of polymer clay, any color for the outline & backing

Quarter block of polymer clay, any color for the center

Parchment paper

24" length of beading wire

3 large jump rings

4 crimp beads

Clasp

Assorted glass beads

Cookie sheet

Tools

Pliers or crimping tool

Cookie sheet

Scissors or wire

Pasta machine

Cutting blade

Ruler

Sharp craft cutter

Oven thermometer

Hole tool or needle

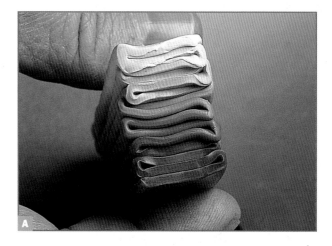

A

MAKING A SKINNER BLEND

1. Condition two colors of polymer clay and shape each color into a rectangle that is one and one-half times as long as it is wide. The width is determined by the width of your pasta machine.

2. Cut each rectangle in half on the diagonal and place one half over the other so that they align.

3. Next, align the two colors so that they form a new rectangle with the edges butted up against each other. Squeeze the edges together so they won't come apart in the next step.

4. Run the rectangle carefully through the pasta machine on setting #1.

5. Fold the rectangle in half in the middle of the length, matching the edges as closely as possible. Flatten the fold to remove any air bubbles.

6. Run the clay through the pasta machine folded-edge first. Repeat 15-20 times until the colors grade smoothly into each other.

MAKING THE MILLEFIORE FLOWERS

1. Condition the half blocks of clay and make a Skinner blend. (See sidebar for instructions.)

2. Fold the Skinner blend in half in the other direction and put it through the pasta machine, leading with the light edge and the dark edge on top. Fold in half length-wise and repeat to create a long, thin Skinner blend.

3. Fan-fold the Skinner blend to form a graduated color block. (See photo A.)

4. Condition a quarter block of a darker color for an outline and put it through the thinnest setting you can manage on your pasta machine.

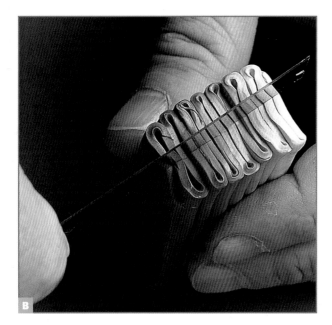

5 Cut the graduated color block three times. Insert the outline color starting at the dark end and continuing until just before you get to the light end, and then reassemble to form the beginning of a petal. (See photo B.)

6 Roll the block until it becomes round, then wrap this piece three-fourths of the way around with the clay you've chosen to be your outside color, leaving both ends uncovered. Pinch into a petal shape.

7 Pull the cane out to about 18 inches, maintaining the petal shape, with the point at the dark end.

8 Cut the cane into six 3-inch pieces. Gently assemble the pieces into a flower with six-petals.

9 Make the flower's center with a simple log of clay. Another fun option is to make a spiral cane by laying a thin sheet of darker clay on top of a thicker sheet of light-colored clay and rolling them into a spiral. Continue rolling until it fits. (See photo C.)

10 Put the center in place and reassemble the flower.

11 Gently pull the cane until it's about 8 inches long.

12 Cut three thin pieces of the flower and two thick pieces. Make holes through the thick slices from one side of the flower through to the opposite side with the needle.

13 Lay the thin slices touching each other in a slight curve on a thick sheet of clay.

14 Trim away the excess clay with the sharp craft-cutting tool. Poke holes at the edge of a petal at either end.

15 Place all pieces on cookie sheet on parchment paper and bake according to manufacturer's instructions.

MAKING THE NECKLACE

1 When your clay pieces have cooled, put two large jump rings in the ends of the centerpiece.

2 Using crimps and beading wire, attach about 12 inches to each side of the centerpiece.

3 String each side with any beads you find pleasing, along with the two thick slices, one on each side.

4 Using crimps, attach a clasp and ring. Enjoy!

Designer: **Sheilah Cleary**

LACY SEED BEAD LARIAT

Victorian ladies made beaded necklaces for themselves using tiny seed beads. You can be just as skilled. When you've mastered the technique (and it won't take long), make a longer lariat, a choker, or a bracelet!

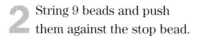

You Will Need

Materials

| Size B nylon beading thread |
| 50 grams size 9, 10 or 11 seed beads |
| 2 10mm decorative beads |
| Beeswax |
| Clear nail polish |

Tools

| Beading needle |

MAKING THE BEAD LACE

1 Cut 54 inches of thread, wax it, and thread onto the needle. Tie a stop bead with a single knot, leaving a 6-inch tail.

2 String 9 beads and push them against the stop bead.

3 Pass needle through (PNT) the second from last bead (bead #8) to make the edge picot.

4 String three beads and PNT the fourth bead from the beginning (not counting the stop bead (bead #4 of the original 9). This bead is a "go through" bead.

5 String three beads and PNT the second from last bead, creating a new edge picot on the other side. Turn the work.

6 String three beads and PNT the center bead of the group

of three from the first row (the beads strung in step 4).

7 When the "lace" is about 7-8 inches long, it will be time to add a new thread. To add a new thread, pull the needle off the first thread after passing through a "go through" bead.

8 Thread a new piece of waxed thread 54 inches long. Tie a small knot in the end and seal it with a tiny drop of nail polish and trim the end. Bring the new needle through the three previous beads and the "go through" bead. Tie the two threads together with a square knot, and seal

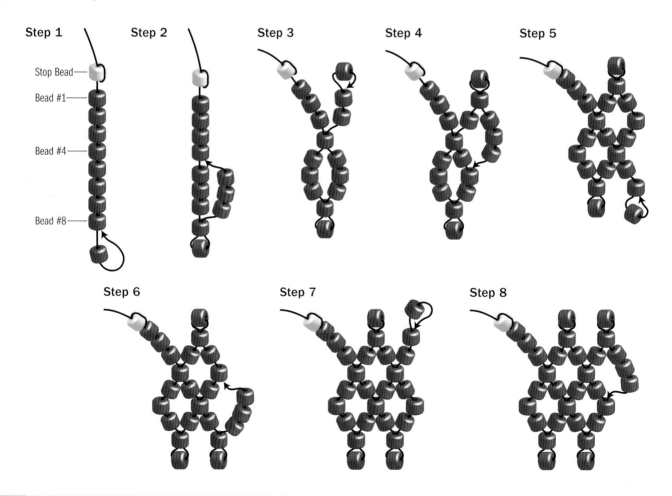

the knot with a drop of nail polish. Continue beading. (Later, you will sew in the ends of the threads as needed.)

9 Repeat rows five and six until desired length. When desired length is reached, complete the picot on the opposite side of the beginning "stop" bead. Pick up three beads and "go through" the center bead, and pull up all the slack. End off the thread by knotting a half hitch and sealing the knot with nail polish. Go through several more beads and do one more half hitch and seal with nail polish. Go through several more beads and clip the thread.

MAKING THE BEAD TASSEL

1 Thread 72 inches of waxed thread and reverse the end-off process to begin the new thread and come out at the center bead.

2 Pick up the decorative bead and place the necklace on the table. Pick up 35 inches of beads.

3 Measure out 7 inches from the decorative bead, leaving a 3-inch space. Lay out another 7 inches of beads. Repeat until there are five sections of beads separated by 3 inches of space laying flat on the table.

4 Carefully loop the empty spaces over your finger, making sure all the loops are the same size

Color Variation

and that there is no extra slack. Wrap the end of the thread around the spots where the beads are separated and then run the needle through the threads, piercing them.

5 Pass the needle up back through the decorative bead and pull up so that there is a shank and the bead tassel is snug against the decorative bead.

6 Run the thread through the center bead and several more beads. Knot with a half hitch and seal with nail polish. Go through several more beads, tie another half hitch, and seal with nail polish. Finally, run through several more beads and clip the thread.

7 Repeat steps 1 through 7 for the tassel on the other end.

TIPS | DIY Network Crafts

Add Color!
Consider using a second, bright, sparkling color for the beads on the tips of the picots and sprinkled through the tassel. Imagine the zest it will give you when it's wrapped around your neck! Just remember to use the colors you like best.

◢ Designer: **Bethany Barry** ◣

FILIGREE NECKLACE

This feminine necklace combines different shapes, colors, textures, and an original center bead that you're going to make yourself!

You Will Need

Materials

69-weight upholstery thread

7-9 large-holed pewter, glass, or Balinese silver beads

A selection of beads in complementary or contrasting colors and sizes*

Center focal bead

Macramé or foam core design board

T-pins

Nail polish or fray-checking solution

Beeswax

*Good bead choices for this project include 6/0 and 8/0 seed beads; small accent beads such as triangles, squares, small faceted Austrian crystal ovals, rondelles, magatamas, daggers, etc; medium-sized accent beads such as 6-8mm glass-like polymer, Czech glass, leaves, flowers, etc. Be sure the bead holes are large enough to allow the thread to pass through.

Tools

Needle

Scissors

Mandrel (or knitting needle or skewer)

STRINGING THE NECKLACE

1 Cut four strands of thread, each about three times as long as the finished necklace. (There is no clasp, so the finished necklace needs to be more than 25 inches long.) Knot all four strands together in an overhand knot at one end, leaving about four inches as a tail. Tack this onto the design board with a T-pin to hold it in place.

2 Cut the opposite ends of the strands at an angle and dip them into nail polish or a fray-checking solution and allow them to dry for five minutes.

3 Begin designing by doing a tentative layout of the beads, thinking about where the colors and shapes will lay in the necklace. Each section of the necklace will be about 4 to

5 inches long. Pewter or accent beads with larger holes divide the sections.

4 Take the first strand of thread, make an overhand knot, string on a bead or charm, make another knot, and leave a ¼-inch space before the next knot, bead, knot. If the knot will slip through the bead, frame the bead with smaller beads on either side. Continue until the first section is complete and pin it aside. Repeat with the remaining three strands of thread, making sure that the beads and knots are staggered when they lie next to the other strands to create a lacy, filigree look.

5 When all four strands are completed for the section, knot them together with a big overhand knot, then run all four strands through a large-holed bead, and make a second large overhand knot. Pin the section in place on the design board. The design board helps you make decisions about symmetry, balance, and color.

6 Continue making sections of the necklace (as in step 4) until half of the necklace is complete. Make an overhand knot with all four strands, take them through a large-holed bead and then through the focal bead and a second large-holed bead, and tie another overhand knot. Continue up the other side of the necklace, repeating the design theme of the first side.

7 When the necklace is complete, combine all eight strands of thread and knot them together. Run them through the bead with the biggest hole, the "back bead", and make a second overhand knot to hold it in place. String small beads on the end of each strand and finish the ends with a double knot for security. Add a drop of glue or nail polish and cut off the extra thread. Staggering the length of the ends makes for a more interesting look.

MAKING A FOCAL COBWEB-WOVEN BEAD

You can create one-of-a-kind focal beads with this easy technique. The beads look great in projects suck as the necklace at left.

1 Cut one very long piece of thread and wax it on both sides, then thread the needle.

2 String on an even number of 8/0 seed beads (enough to encircle the mandrel). Connect the ends together, leaving a 6-inch tail to be woven in later. Place the bead circle on the mandrel and tape the tail to anchor it to the mandrel.

3 Using the one-drop Peyote stitch, make a bead tube about 12 rows or 1½ inches long.

4 Needle out through a bead, pick up four to six seed beads, and go across the surface of the tube at an angle. Put the needle through another bead in the base and come out the other side. Pick up more beads and go across at another angle, working in a criss-cross fashion. Continue weaving back and forth until the bead base is covered with crosses.

5 For the next layer, pick up more beads, including accent beads (for example, two 11/0s, a small accent bead, and two more 11/0s). Weave these beads across the surface, going through base beads as before, and filling in all the spaces to create a colorful, sculptural effect.

6 Weave the two ends of the thread back into the beads, hide the thread and tie it off. Run the ends a little further in, and trim the excess.

7 Remove the bead from the mandrel and place it front and center in your necklace.

TIPS | DIY Network Crafts

Knots and Pins
Keep the knot loops loose until the beads are in position so they'll be easy to adjust. Put a T-pin in the knot to hold it taut next to its bead.

Designer: **Anne Mitchell**

LEATHER & JUMP RING BRACELET

This bold and funky bracelet design is perfect for men and women. All it takes is a long length of leather cord and a handful of jump rings.

You Will Need

Materials

- 80" length of 1.5mm leather cord
- 48" length of 24-gauge sterling silver wire
- 1 Troy ounce 16-gauge jump rings, 5.5mm inside diameter
- ½ Troy ounce 16-gauge jump rings, 6.5mm inside diameter
- 4-5 beads with holes large enough to fit over ten strands of leather
- Large, soldered, 16-gauge wire jump ring, 7mm inside diameter
- Pair of sterling silver cone end pieces
- Swivel clasp

Tools

- Chain-nose pliers
- Bent chain-nose pliers
- Round-nose pliers
- Nylon-jaw wire straightening pliers
- Wire cutters
- Velvet pad work surface
- #2 pencil

MAKING THE BRACELET

1 Cut the leather cord into eight 10-inch lengths and the silver wire into four 12-inch lengths.

2 Bend two 12-inch sections of wire in half. Bend the other two sections of 12-inch wire at the inch mark into a 90-degree angle.

3 Hold one piece of wire with a 90-degree bend and a piece of leather together, positioning the wire about 2 inches in from the end of the leather with the short end of the wire facing toward the short end of the leather. Wrap the long end twice around the 1-inch leg of wire and the piece of leather. (See photo A.)

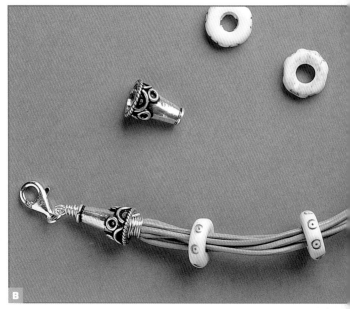

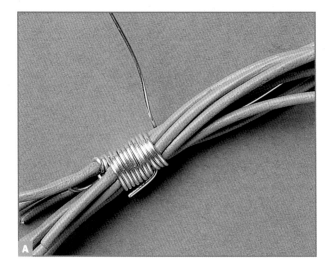

4 Position a piece of the bent wire around the leather and gather the remaining seven pieces of leather around the leather/wire piece you assembled in step 3.

5 Check to be sure the doubled wire ends are protruding from the eight bundled strands of leather and that the 90-degree angle wire is protruding from the bundle. Wrap the 90-degree wire toward the short end of the leather bundle for ½ inch, wrapping tightly and without gaps.

6 Trim off the excess leather at the top of the wire wrap, taking care not to cut off the two strands of silver wire protruding from the end of the bundle.

7 Place the silver cone onto the silver wires and the end of the bundle.

8 Wire wrap the soldered jump ring onto the end of the silver cone with the two strands of protruding wire.

9 Place the large diameter beads onto the leather bundle. (See photo B.)

10 Place the leather bundle around your wrist to get an accurate measurement for the bracelet's size; mark the leather with a pencil. Start the wire wrap at the pencil mark to ensure the correct size of the bracelet.

11 Repeat steps two through six at the other end of the bracelet. Repeat step seven with the swivel clasp instead of the soldered jump ring.

12 Place jump rings around leather in an interesting pattern, alternating the two sizes for variety.

Designer: **Ana Araujo**

SHELL BRACELET

It's the mermaid clasp that makes this bracelet entirely oceanic! Spend some time laying out the design, then you can incorporate other colors and beads. Experiment with square crystals, saltwater pearls, shells of different shapes, and even silver charms!

MAKING THE BRACELET

1 Fold a 28-inch length of beading wire in half.

2 Loop over one end of the toggle.

You Will Need

Materials

Nylon-coated beading wire, .025mm diameter, in a light or bronze color

Round shells

4mm bicone Austrian crystals (clear blue, peach AB, and sea glass colored)

6mm pewter cast beads

Square Paula shells

#3 Crimp/Spacer Tubes

Mermaid toggle clasp

Tools

Flush cutter

Crimping pliers

Tweezers with shovel attachment

20" straight channel bead board

3 Place a crimp tube over both ends of the wire, slide up to the toggle end, and crimp.

4 Slide a clear blue crystal over one strand of wire and run the other strand through the crystal from the other direction. Pull snugly. (See photo A.)

5 Slide a peach crystal on the right wire and one onto the left wire.

6 Slide on a pewter cast bead over both wires.

7 Slide on round shell over both wires.

8 Slide on a pewter cast bead over both wires.

9 Slide a peach crystal on the right wire and one onto the left wire.

10 Slide a sea glass crystal on the right wire.

11 Place the left wire through the hole, then pull both wires tight.

12 Slide a bugle bead on the right wire and one on the left.

13 Slide a Paula Shell over both wires.

14 Slide a bugle iris bead on the right wire and one on the left.

15 Repeat the pattern from the top until the bracelet is the right length.

16 Slide the crimp tube over both wires. Loop both wires over the toggle, back through the crimp tube, and then through a couple of the beads. (See photo B.)

17 Crimp snugly with the crimping pliers and clip off any excess wire.

A

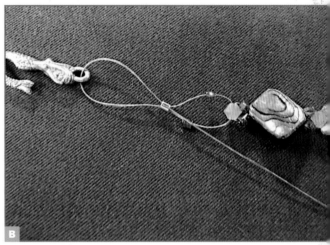

B

TIPS | DIY Network Crafts

Hot Tip

Sea shells are the theme for this bracelet, but if you're more an earth mother than a mermaid, adjust the materials to suit yourself. Use a different color scheme, wooden beads, and some wonderful gemstones like agate or unakite with mystical properties that will enhance your beautiful inner self.

◀ Designer: **Janet Pitcher** ▶

BUTTERFLY NECKLACE

Once you've mastered these simple steps for working with polymer clay, you'll be ready to unleash your creativity by adding butterflies, flowers, and beads to your necklaces, bracelets and earrings. It's a project for almost every age of jewelry maker!

You Will Need

Materials

2-ounce polymer clay block in four colors (Purple, fuchsia, green, and yellow were used in the project shown here.)

4-ounce block of white polymer clay

Beading wire and closure or elastic beading string and strong bonding glue

Tools

Pasta machine

Tissue blade for slicing

Dedicated toaster oven/ oven thermometer (home oven may be used)

Skewers for piercing beads

Non-porous work surface such as a ceramic tile

▒ MAKING THE BEADS ▒

1 Condition the clay by kneading it well, then run it through the pasta machine several times on the largest setting.

2 Blend 1 ounce purple clay with ½ ounce white to create lavender, folding and running the clay through the pasta machine until the color is consistent. Roll on thickest setting into rectangle approximately 2½ by 3 inches.

3 Prepare the medium-pink color by blending one ounce fuchsia clay with one ounce white. Roll on the pasta machine's thickest setting into rectangle approximately 2½ by 3 inches.

4 Prepare the lime green color by blending ¼ ounce green clay with 1 ounce yellow. Roll on the pasta machine's thickest setting into rectangles approximately 2½ inches by 3 inches.

5 Lay the three rectangles on top of each other in the following order: green, then lavender, then pink. Square off the rectangle by slicing off the excess clay to measure 2½ inches by 3 inches.

6 Flatten the layered rectangle by pressing on the short end then begin rolling like a jellyroll.

7 Roll lightly on the work surface, moving your fingers outward to reduce the cane to about ½ inch in diameter. Cut length of cane in half, then reduce one of the halves by rolling to about ¼ inch in diameter.

8 To make the butterfly's wings, cut two slices about ¼-inch thick from each end of the ½- and ¼-inch diameter canes. Position the slices in a mirror image to create the wings. Lightly press the top and bottom wings together.

9 Create a support bead with green clay by forming a rectangle about ¾ by ½ inches and ¼-inch thick. Gently press the wings onto this base.

10 For the body, roll a small ball of green, purple or pink clay and into a snake. Place the body at the center of the wings. Press lightly to secure. Pierce a hole with small skewer through the top half of the rectangle.

11 Make accent beads using the rest of the canes, referring to the sidebar. (See photo.)

12 Bake beads following the manufacturer's instructions in a well-ventilated area. Remove from oven and cool.

13 String cooled beads on beading wire with closure; alternatively, string beads on elastic beading string, then tie a knot and secure with strong bonding glue.

MAKING ACCENT BEADS

- An incredible variety of accent beads can be made with these simple techniques. Have fun!

- Slice 5mm beads, then pierce a threading hole with skewer.

- Slice thin pieces from a cane and lay on a solid-colored bead. Roll in hands to smooth into ball, then pierce a threading hole with skewer.

- Roll a covered ball into cylinder shaped bead, then add contrasting end caps. Pierce with skewer.

- Make flower bead by arranging five small jellyrolls lengths of cane around a solid green center log. Slice and pierce as directed above.

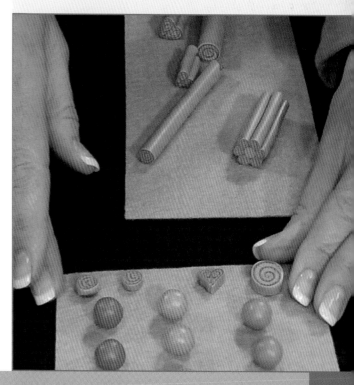

Designer: **Sheilah Cleary**

CRYSTAL WATCH BAND

Why shouldn't your watchband sparkle as much as the rest of your jewelry? It should, and it can! All you need is some beading wire and a handful of crystals in your favorite colors.

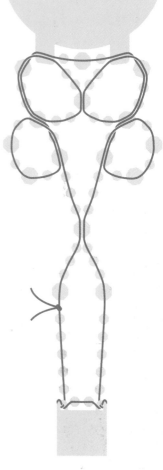

You Will Need

Materials

50" of .010 nylon-coated beading wire

A watch face with two attachments

Approximately 110 2mm or 3mm crystals in several pastel colors

30 5mm crystals

Two-hole clasp

Tools

Wire cutter

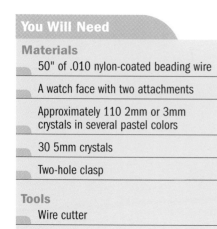

BEADING THE WATCHBAND

1 Cut a 12-inch length of beading wire, then thread the wire through one of the holes in the watch face from the outside toward the other hole on the same side.

2 String a 3mm, a 5mm, and a 3mm crystal on the wire and pass it through the other hole.

3 Following the schematic, string the beads for the first side one to the last 5mm crystal as marked. (See photos A and B.)

4 Repeat for the second half of the watchband.

5 Pass the wire through one side of the clasp and string two 3mm crystals.

6 Pass the wire through the second hole in the clasp.

7 String the remaining crystals for side one.

8 Tie a knot in the beading wire.

9 Pass one wire through the 5mm crystal, pull the wire until the knot pops into the bead.

10 Pass the second wire in the opposite direction through several crystals.

11 Trim the wires close to the crystals, then repeat steps 1 through 10 for the other side of the watchband.

diy
network

3

Wire Wrapping

Wire is a great gift to jewelry making! As a technique, wire wrapping definitely a takes some practice. Once you get the hang of it, though, you'll be dazzled by what you can make with just a length of wire, two pairs of pliers, and your imagination! You can make dangles, connectors, clasps, ear wires, and almost everything else in the jewelry world. The simplest technique is a simple loop, which turns a head pin and a bead into a dangle. Add coils to the stem of a dangle for beauty and reinforcement. The coils can become beads themselves, or a piece of wire and a bead can become the link in a chain. Given the variety of types and sizes of wire sold today, the possibilities are endless. Remember: wire, two pair of pliers, and a dash of you is the recipe to make something beautiful!

Designer: **Jackie Guerra**

ANTIQUE BUTTON EARRINGS

The tiny mother-of-pearl buttons on antique clothing can be as perfect a jewel as anything in a bead store. Don't let them get away! Recycle them into a delicate pair of feminine earrings.

You Will Need

Materials:

- 2 small mother-of-pearl buttons
- 16-gauge gold French leverback ear wires
- 26-gauge gold wire
- 6 fine gold headpins
- 2 small gold jump rings
- 8 3mm bicone crystals
- 2 4mm bicone crystals

Tools:

- HypoCement glue
- Wire cutters
- Round-nose pliers
- Flat-nose pliers
- Jump-ring pliers

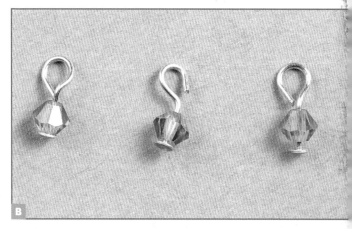

⁓ MAKING THE EARRINGS ⁓

1. Select two small buttons, one for each earring. Two-hole buttons work best.

2. Cut two 2-inch lengths of gold wire. Use round-nose pliers to create two wire-wrapped 3mm crystals with a loop on either side. Don't entirely close the loops; set them aside.

3. Cut two 5-inch lengths of gold wire and run a 4mm crystal on the center of each. With flat-nose pliers, bend a 90-degree turn close to the crystal on each side. Thread each end through a hole in the button and seat the crystal snugly upright on the button. (See photo A.)

4. For each button, bend each end of wire away from the center. Using the round-nose pliers, create a loop with a tail. Wrap the tail around the wire and cut off the excess. Repeat this step for both ends of wire on both buttons.

5. Using the headpins, the remaining 3mm crystals, and the round-nose pliers, create small bead dangles with tiny loops at the top. (See photo B.)

6. Open a jump ring and attach three crystal dangles onto one loop of the button. Repeat for the other button.

7. Link the button to the ear wire with the wire-wrapped crystal from step 2. Be careful that the button hangs from the earwire so that its crystal faces forward. Twist the loops a little if needed.

8. Make sure all the joints stay snug by adding a tiny drop of glue to each.

TIPS | DIY Network Crafts

Buy Extra!

If you're lucky enough to find more than two matching antique buttons, buy them! Use the extras to make a matching bracelet or necklace, or save them to make a matching set of earrings for the first friend who admires them.

network

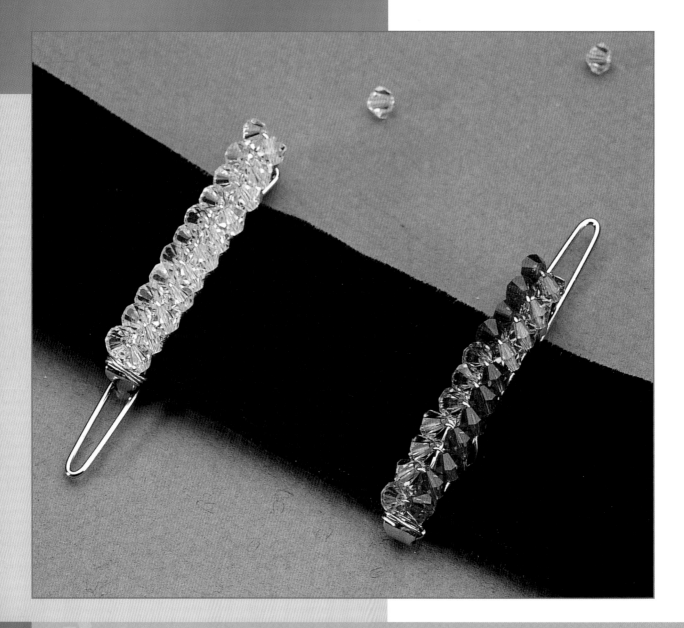

◄ Designer: **Jackie Guerra** ►

BEADED BARRETTES

These fun barrettes are easy to coordinate with
your favorite outfits and are the ideal solution to
bad hair days!

You Will Need

Materials:

¼" x 2" barrette

22 4mm Austrian bicone crystals

18" of half-hard, 24-gauge wire in silver or
gold (match the barrette)

Tools:

Round-nose pliers

Flush-wire cutters

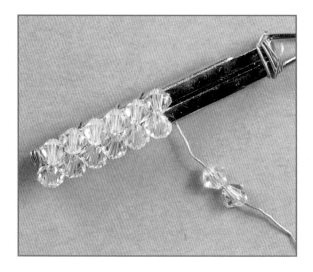

 MAKING THE BARRETTES

1 Wrap four coils of wire snugly and tightly at one end of the open barrette.

2 Thread two crystals onto the wire and wrap them across the top of the barrette, angling them so they nest together with the wire and points touching in the center.

3 Continue wrapping the wire snugly and tightly. The crystals should be positioned consistently and will create a pavée effect across the top of the barrette. (See photo.)

4 At the end of the barrette, tightly wrap four coils of wire. Clip the wire, then tuck it so that it doesn't tangle in hair.

TIPS | DIY Network Crafts

Sparkling Inspiration
Swarovski crystals have inspired thousands of handcrafted jewelry pieces. For your own unique creations, string patterns of crystal beads onto wire, then bend them into fun shapes and forms. Finish with a pin backing to create one-of-a-kind brooches.

JACKIE'S BEADED HEADBAND

For another dazzling way to keep the hair out of your eyes, try beading a headband, which you can find in hair supply stores. I guarantee people will stop you on the street to find out where you got your crowning achievement!

You Will Need

Materials:
Pronged wire headband

Approximately 200 4mm Austrian bicone crystals

48" of 24-gauge half-hard wire

Tools:
Round-nose pliers

Wire cutters

1 Loop one end of the wire around the first prong of the headband, taking care to keep the prongs away from your face as you work.

2 Loop the wire around the anchor (the first prong) at least three or four times.

3 Install two crystals onto the headband. Bend the wire around the first and second prong while holding the crystals with your index finger. (Also be sure to hold your index finger on the wire.)

4 Pull the wire tight to hold the crystals snugly in place, then continue adding pairs of crystals above each prong on the headband. (Depending upon how the prongs are spaced apart, you may have room for an extra wire wrap or more crystals.)

Once you complete the headband, anchor the wire down onto the last prong three or four times and snip away the excess wire with wire cutters.

Designer: **Orna Willis**

PROM EARRINGS

When you've gotten the perfect gown for your prom, wedding or other special event, you need the perfect matching, chandelier earrings!

You Will Need

Materials:

6 aqua-colored 4mm Czech glass beads (A)

8 aqua-colored 4mm Swarovski crystals (B)

10 3mm silver smooth round beads (C)

8 5mm square silver spacer beads (D)

24 silver-soldered 3mm jump rings (E)

6 blue topaz 8mm briolettes (F)

6 4mm "Jade" Peridot round beads (G)

5mm silver coils (H)

Delica Sea Blue Luster beads (I)

Delica Chartreuse beads (J)

4" silver head pins

Pair silver ear wires

24-gauge silver wire

2 5mm silver open jump rings

Tools:

Round-nose pliers

Flat-nose pliers

Jewelry wire cutters

MAKING THE EARRINGS

1 Wire wrap the briolettes to prepare them for hanging, referring to the directions in the sidebar.

2 Starting at the head end of a head pin, prepare the center hanging piece by threading beads in the following sequence: A, E (3x), B, E, G, E, B, E (3x), C. After beading the headpin, cut off excess head pin leaving ¼" of wire. Form loop using round-nose pliers.

3 Thread another head pin in the following sequence, starting from the head of the pin: H, A, I, J, I, D, B, D, I, J, I, C, briolette, C, I, J, I, E, G, E, B, briolette; next, reverse the order working back to H.

4 Form a loop at the end of the head pin. Cut off the head of the pin and form a loop on that end. Turn the loops so that they face each other as shown.

5 Flip over the head pin with beads and briolettes. Using a thumbnail, press down on the head pin at the point of the middle briolette, bending the two sides upward.

6 Place your thumb at the point right before the side briolettes, one at a time, bending the wire out to the sides. Then, right after the briolettes, press down again, bending the wire toward the top, meeting the loops on the ends of the wire. (See Bending the Earrings.)

7 Position the center hanging piece you prepared between the two loops of the earring head pin, lining up the holes of the loops. Connect the three loops with a jump ring, then attach to the loop of an ear wire.

8 Repeat steps 1 through 7 for the second earring.

Bending the Earrings

Step 1

Step 2

Step 3

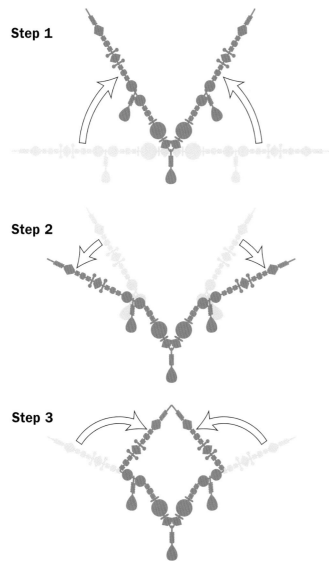

WIRE WRAPPING BRIOLETTE DANGLES

1 Use the round-nose pliers to slightly bend the loop at the top of the wire. The finished piece will look like a coat hanger, and this is the neck of the hanger.

2 Use the flat-nose pliers to grasp the head pin next to the neck of the hanger. Bend the tail to form the bottom of the hanger.

3 Thread the briolette onto the hanger.

4 Use the round-nose pliers to hold the hanger at the neck and the flat-nose pliers to bend the tail of the head pin up and over toward the neck.

5 Use the round-nose pliers to grip the two top wires of the hanger close to the briolette and grab the tip of the head pin tail. Wrap it around the neck of the hanger.

6 Trim off any excess wire and check to be sure the cut end of the wire is snug and smooth at the neck of the hanger.

◢ Designer: **Shari Bonnin** ◣

FLOWER BOBBY PINS

Isn't it great when something really functional is also really beautiful? Fill your hair with these sparkling flowers that double as bobby pins.

You Will Need

Materials:

2' length of 26-gauge wire

7 6mm glass beads

8mm glass pearl

2 glass leaf beads, drilled sideways like briolettes

Small bobby pin

Tools:

Chain-nose pliers

Wire cutters

MAKING THE BOBBY PINS

1 String the 6mm beads onto the wire and thread the wire through the four beginning beads to form a tight circle. Leave a 6- to 8-inch tail at one end.

2 Put the pearl on the long end of the wire and fold the wire down to the tail. The pearl should sit in the center of the flower.

3 Wrap the long end of wire up and away from the short end of the wire. Wrap it over the wire between every two beads, turning the flower as you go. Because there are an odd number of beads, you won't wrap the same place twice. Keep wrapping until a six-sided star of wire appears on both sides of the flower. You should end at the point where the short tail is. Twist the wires together twice. (See photo A.)

4 Place the top of the flower on the top of the bobby pin where it opens. The loop end of the bobby pin becomes the bottom of the flower "stalk." Wrap the wires around the top side of the bobby pin twice. (Remember to wrap the wire around the top prong of the bobby pin, not both!)

5 Add a leaf to the wires and twist them around the bobby pin twice. Add the second leaf on the other side of the "stalk," twisting twice. (See photo B.)

6 Twist the wire around the short portion of the bobby pin three to four times toward the base of the bobby pin. Cut the wire, then use chain-nose pliers to make sure the wire ends are flat and snug.

Designer: **Kate Ferrant-Richbourg**

STACKED WIRE CUFF

If you choose your materials with a designer's eye, materials such as coiled silver, pearls, crystals, and beads can be combined to create an elegant cuff bracelet.

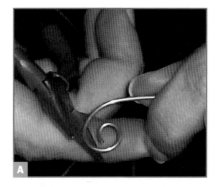

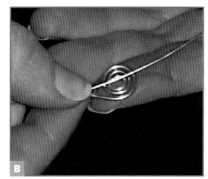

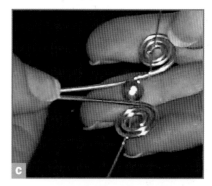

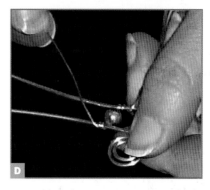

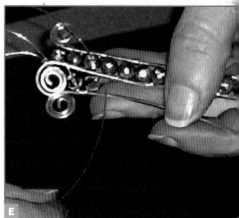

MAKING THE CUFF

1 Cut the 16-gauge wire into four 12-inch lengths, then cut the 24-gauge wire into three 18-inch lengths. (Note: A two-tier cuff will use three lengths of 16-gauge wire, while a three-tier cuff uses four.)

2 Use a tape measure to measure your wrist. The tape measure should fit snugly around the wrist. Add ¼ to ½ of an inch to this measurement.

3 Make one spiral end on each of two pieces of the 16-gauge wire. These heavy wires will form the base of the cuff. The spiral can be any size and any diameter since its purpose is decorative. (See photo A.)

4 Securely wrap the 24-gauge wire around one of the 16-gauge wires about three times. (See photo B.) String a bead onto the 24-gauge wire and wrap the wire around the second 16-gauge base wire three times to secure the bead between the two wires. The bead will sit at a slight angle between the wires. (See photos C and D.)

5 Continue adding the beads until the length is ½ to ¾ inches shorter than the finished desired length. End the wrapping by cutting the wire away after the last wrap and tucking in the end.

6 To add another tier, use a new 16-gauge wire with a spiraled end and wrap between the existing finished piece and the new wire. (See photo E.)

7 Repeat for a third tier.

8 To shape the cuff, carefully bend cuff into a curve on a large dowel or mandrel to fit the wrist.

9 Finish the open ends of the base wires by making a spiral on each, then fine-tune the curve of the cuff.

Designer: **Michele DeFay**

CHANDELIER EARRINGS

A little bit of wire, a little bit of chain, a few beautiful stones, and a pair of ear wires is all you need for an elegant pair of chandelier earrings.

You Will Need

Materials:

15" 22-gauge sterling silver half-hard wire

2 sterling silver ear wires

8" fine silver chain

2 faceted briolettes

16 4mm aventurine smooth round beads

8 2x4 aventurine smooth tube beads

Tools:

Round-nose pliers

Wire cutters

MAKING THE EARRINGS

1 Measure and cut a 2-inch length of silver wire. Attach one end of silver wire to one ear wire with a wrapped loop.

2 String a round bead onto the ear wire.

3 Attach the ear wire below the bead to the center of a 4-inch length of chain using a wrapped loop. Trim off any excess wire.

4 Thread a faceted briolette onto a 3-inch length of silver wire. String a round bead, a tube bead, and a second round bead onto both sides of the briolette. (See photo A.)

5 Attach each end of the wire to each end of the chain using a wrapped loop. Trim off any excess wire.

6 String alternating aventurine tube beads and round beads on a 3-inch length of wire.

7 Find the center point of the chain between the ear wire and the pendant. Attach the wire with five beads to each side of the chain at the center point using a wrapped loop on each side. Trim off any excess wire. (See photo B.)

8 Repeat steps 1-7 to make a second earring. Carefully bend the wires to curve downward into gentle swags.

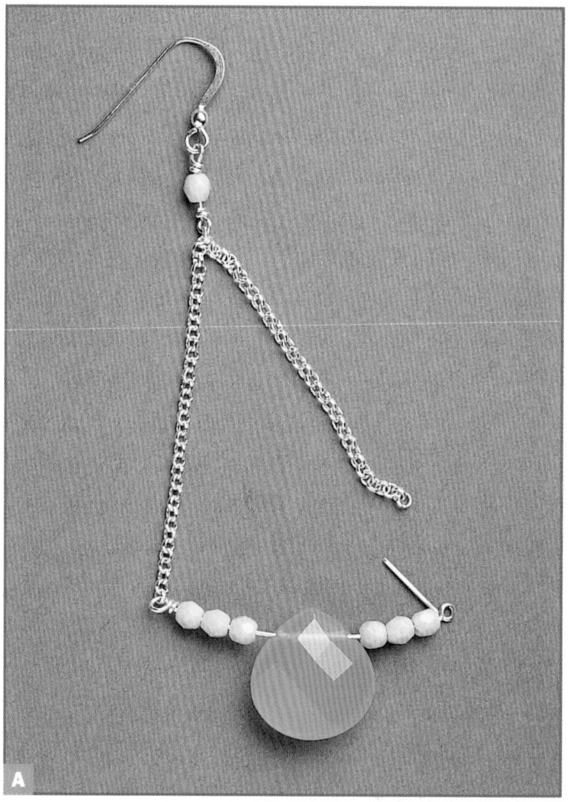
A

B

TIPS | DIY Network Crafts

Chandelier Variations

As you make this project, you will quickly realize that it's easy to alter the earring's design. You can make the chain longer and add additional wires with gemstones between them. For a matching necklace, create an extra chandelier and wear it on a simple chain. As always, use the projects in this book to jump start your own unique creativity!

▶ Designer: **Akiko Masuda** ▶

WIRE-WRAPPED RING

With only two elements — wire and gemstones — you can create a stunning ring. Just don't tell your friends how easy it was to make!

You Will Need

Materials:

50" of 24-gauge sterling silver wire

Small gemstone chips, pearls, and beads

Tools:

Wire cutters

Ring size mandrel (Optional)

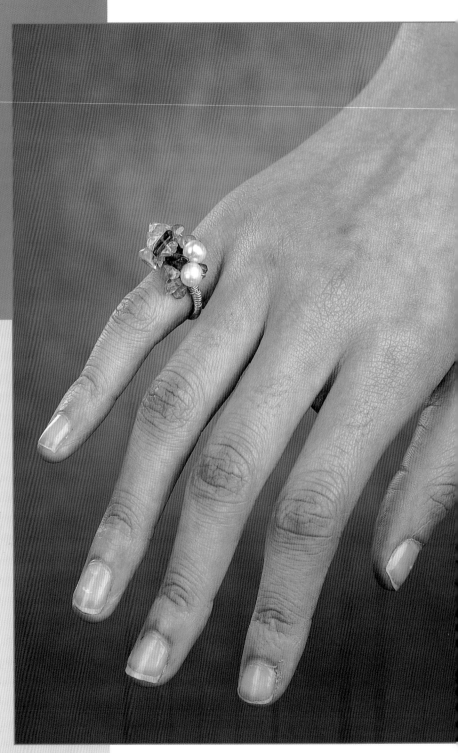

MAKING THE RING

1 With one end of the wire, measure the size of your finger and add one half inch. Fold four times until there are five strands of wire together, with extra wire on one end. (See photo A.)

2 Hold the five folded pieces of wire together (this is the ring base) and coil the remaining wire snugly onto these folded wires, making sure to leave a small hoop at the end of the ring base. (See photo B.)

3 Leave another hoop at the other end of the ring base and insert the end of the remaining wire into the first hoop. Leave about ⅛ inch of wire separating the two hoops. This piece is the stone base.

4 On the remaining length of wire, thread two or three peridot chips and wrap the end of the wire through the center around the stone base. (See photo C.)

5 Repeat until you are satisfied with the cluster of stones on the ring.

6 To finish, cut off the remaining wire, leaving about ¼ inch still attached to the ring. Wrap the excess wire around the ring base and hide its end in the stone cluster.

7 Make sure the ring fits and is perfectly round by pushing it down onto a dowel the size of your finger or on the ring mandrel.

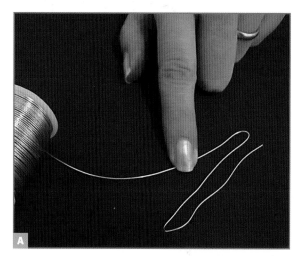

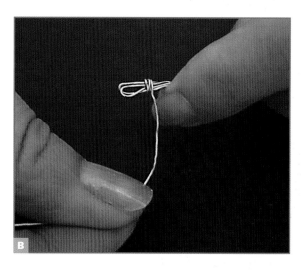

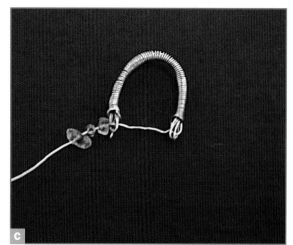

TIPS | DIY Network Crafts

Go Shopping!

You'd be amazed at the findings and finishings you'll be able to find by surfing the internet. There are ring bases of all sorts, many of which include loops on the top. With these, you can attach the stones as dangles, which will give you a floppier look and some movement.

◤ Designer: **Doris Coghill** ◢

GROWING VINE NECKLACE

This free-form necklace will look different every time you make it! The spacing and length of the clusters, as well as the types of beads you choose, create unique, fun combinations.

You Will Need

Materials:

Focal bead

20" of nylon-coated beading wire, size .014

26-gauge wire (color of your choice)

4 crimp tubes

Assortment of flower and leaf beads

Larger leaf bead or other center focal piece

Assortment of size 6 seed beads, 6mm glass beads, 4mm glass beads, and various accent beads or crystals

Clasp

2 split rings

Tools:

Protective goggles or eyeglasses

Wire cutters

Flat-nose pliers

Crimping pliers

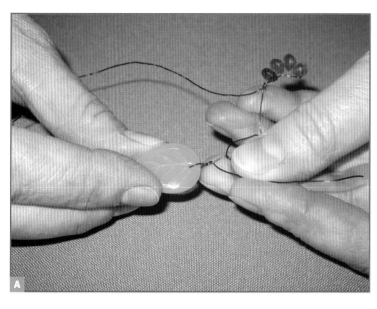

A

MAKING THE NECKLACE

1 Cut the beading wire into two even lengths and the 26-gauge wire into one 2-yard length and one 3-yard length.

2 Slide the focal bead to the center of the 3-yard length of wire. Twist the wire close to the bead for ⅛ to ¼ inch twist. (To twist, hold the bead firmly in one hand and twist with the other hand.) Note that all the twists in the necklace should be twisted in the same direction. (See photo A.)

3 Add several bead clusters to each wire, with each cluster spaced less than ¼ inch apart and with a ⅛- to ¼-inch stem on each cluster. See sidebar for clustering techniques.

4 After every two or three clusters, twist the individual clusters together to give the piece body and keep the clusters closer together. (See photo B, next page.)

5 When 1 or 2 inches of clusters are twisted together on each side of the focal bead, decide which side will be the front of the necklace and arrange the clusters so that the beads are facing the front. You now have completed the focal section of the necklace.

6 Add the second piece of wire by twisting the center of it around the wires directly behind the focal section. There should now be two ends of wire going up each side of the necklace.

Continued on page 70.

ADDING BEAD CLUSTERS

Single Bead Cluster: Add a bead and slide it into its final position, taking care to leave enough room to wrap the wires together under the bead. Fold the wire back and down along the side of the bead. Twist the two pieces of wire together directly under the bead for about ¼ inch to form a stem.

Multiple Bead Cluster: This cluster is made the same way as the single bead cluster, except than an odd number of multiple beads are added at once. Form the wire into a loop shape following the shape of the beads, twisting the end together while keeping the first and last beads together at the bottom of the loop. (Be sure to leave enough room to wrap the wires together under the bead.)

Fringe Stitch Cluster: This cluster is constructed just like a sewn fringe on a necklace, except using wire. String one to four beads on the wire and slide them down into their permanent position, leaving enough room to wrap the wires together. Skipping the top bead, put the wire back down through the other beads. Pull the wire tight while making sure to hold the beads in their final positions. Twist the two pieces of wire around each other for about ¼ inch, forming a stem.

7 Continue adding bead clusters, twisting after each one, until the necklace is the desired length. You can make these clusters close together or space them further apart.

8 As close as possible to the last cluster, twist the wire for about ¼ inch. Form a small loop with this twisted wire and wrap the end of the wire back around itself. Wrap the end under a couple of sections and cut off the excess wire, making sure the end of the wire is buried so that it will not scratch your skin.

9 Cut a piece of nylon-coated beading wire 2 inches longer than necessary to finish the necklace. String a crimp tube and pass the beading wire through the wire loop and back through the crimp tube. Using crimp pliers, squeeze the crimp tube closed.

10 String enough beads to complete the necklace onto the nylon-coated wire, ending with another crimp tube and a split ring. Pass the wire back through the crimp tube and squeeze the crimp tube closed. Attach the clasp to the split ring.

11 Repeat steps 8 through 10 on the other side of the necklace.

TEST TUBE TUSSIE MUSSIE PIN

Designer:
Chris Franchetti

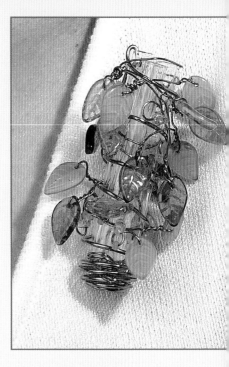

Create contemporary versions of Victorian tussie-mussies with miniature test tubes for faux vases. Add water and a real flower for a charming finish!

MAKING THE PIN

1 Glue the pin back to the test tube with the sharp point of the pin pointing downward. Allow the glue to set overnight.

2 Create a tiny loop in the end of the 20-gauge wire with the round-nose pliers. Using the flat-nose pliers, gently continue coiling the wire until it's just large enough to cover the very bottom of the test tube.

You Will Need

Materials:

6x50mm glass test tube
Pin back
11" of 20-gauge copper wire
21" of 24-gauge copper wire
Green Czech glass leaf bead
13 olive-green 4mm Czech glass faceted beads
13 medium-green seed beads
Jewelry glue

Tools:

Small round-nose pliers
Small flat-nose pliers
Flush wire cutters
Jewelry-making jig

3 Using the tip of the flat-nose pliers, push down on the center of the coil to form a little cup. Place the bottom of the test tube into the cup. Holding the cup securely in place with your fingers, wrap the long end of the wire up around the test tube several times.

4 Wrap the wire around the pin back or through it, making sure the pin back can still close properly. Trim the wire if necessary, then gently fold the end of the wire over the top lip of the test tube. The key to not breaking the tube here is to make sure your pliers only touch the wire, and not the glass, as you make the fold. (See photo A.)

5 Thread the leaf bead onto the 24-gauge wire about 4 inches from one end of the wire. Twist twice to secure it in place.

6 String all but one of the seed beads and all of the 4mm beads onto the longer end of the wire in an alternating pattern (beginning with a seed bead), and fold over the end of the wire so they don't fall off.

7 Arrange all the small pegs in a line on the jig. Starting just past the leaf bead, wrap the wire around the first peg, dropping a seed bead into the new loop. Now drop down a 4mm bead (which will be in the space between loops). Continue creating loops with seed beads, separated by 4mm beads, until all the beads are used. Carefully remove the 24-gauge wire from the jig, closing any loops that have come open. (See photo B.)

8 Create one more beaded loop using the jig or your round-nose pliers on the other side of the leaf bead.

9 Hold the leaf-end of the wire near the top of the test tube, and use your fingers to press the first loop to the side of the tube and place the leaf where you'd like it to rest. Wrap the remaining unbeaded portion of the wire around the top of the test tube once or twice, and secure by wrapping it around the wire leaf "stem" several times. Trim any excess wire.

10 Continue down the test tube, wrapping the beaded loops around the tube and flattening the loops gently along the way. If you wrap through the pin back, be sure to slide the beads out of that area so the pin back will close properly. Secure the 24-gauge wire by wrapping it in with the 20-gauge wire cup at the bottom of the test tube. (See photo C.)

11 Fill the test tube with water using a dropper or slowly running faucet and place a small flower inside. Enjoy!

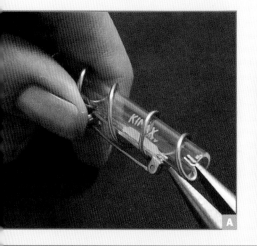

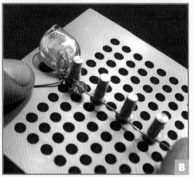

network

◀ Designer: **Beki Haley** ▶

CHARM BRACELET

This charming bracelet makes a great project to practice the wire wrapping. The technique is used to attach the charms in this project, and is one of the basic techniques used in many of the other projects in this chapter.

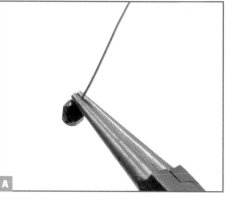

You Will Need

Materials:

Sterling silver chain-link bracelet

Assorted glass beads

Metal beads

Freshwater pearls

Assorted charms

22-gauge sterling silver headpins, 2" long

22-gauge sterling silver open jump rings, 5-6mm

Tools:

Round-nose pliers

Flat-nose pliers

Wire cutters

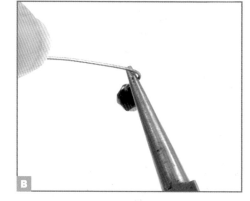

MAKING THE BRACELET

1 Select the beads and charms so that the colors and sizes work well together.

2 Lay out your beads and charms and design the groupings that will go on each headpin. Design each one a little differently for a unique look.

3 Add some charms to the ends of some of the headpins by cutting off the head and making a loop in which to attach the charm.

4 Twist your wire to make a nice professional loop. (See page 17 for a review of the technique and photos A through D for a visual guide.)

5 Lay out your design to keep it uniform and balanced, but not symmetrical.

6 Attach your newly created charms to your bracelet with jump rings.

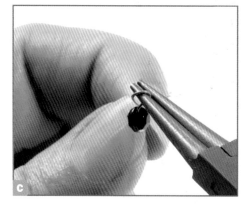

TIPS | DIY Network Crafts

Friendship Bracelet
Looking for a one-of-a-kind gift for someone special? Ask close friends to purchase a unique charm or two and present them in prettily wrapped packages. Afterward, bring all of the charms home and make them into a bracelet that will become a cherished keepsake.

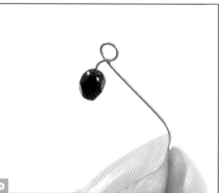

◄ Designer: **Kathy Davis** ►

METAL CLAY
SILVER BEADS

Use these simple techniques to
mold and sculpt silver beads from
metal clay. Once fired, the beads are
pure silver in color and can be used
in dozens of creative ways.

You Will Need

Materials:

Silver clay*

Olive oil

20-gauge sterling silver wire

Silver clay paste

*Read the manufacturer's instructions and
safety tips on working with silver clay paste
and a torch!

Tools:

Rubber stamp

Round-nose pliers

Chain-nose pliers

Flush cutters

Small file

Large syringe (no needle required!)

Small butane torch

Firing brick

Wire brush

Burnisher

MAKING THE BEADS

1 Form the clay into flat, square lumps about ¾ inches across. This shape is larger than the finished bead to allow for eight to ten percent shrinkage when the piece is fired.

2 Brush olive oil lightly onto the rubber stamp and press the stamp into the clay to add texture.

3 Cut pieces of wire into ¼- to ½-inch lengths and bend them into U shapes. Insert the loops of wire into opposite sides of the clay beads.

4 Fill the syringe with clay paste and decorate one or both sides of the bead.

5 Dry completely and sand any problem areas with the small file if necessary. (See photo A.)

6 Place the beads on the firing brick and fire two to three minutes with the torch, following the manufacturer's instructions. (See photo B.)

7 Pick up each piece with pliers and quench it in a large bowl of water.

8 Brush each bead with the wire brush and finish polishing with the burnisher. (See photo C.)

9 The beads are ready to be made into jewelry with the addition of other beads, chain, and findings.

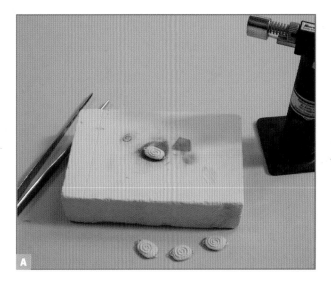

TIPS | DIY Network Crafts

Wrap it up!

Metal clay beads look great with decorative wire-wrapped connectors. Just thread a clay bead onto a length of wire about an inch longer than the bead. Make wire loops on each end of the wire. Repeat with enough bead/wire sections to encircle your wrist, then attach the bead links to each other and add a clasp.

SILVER & CRYSTAL NECKLACE

Here's another way to use your simple wire-wrapping techniques to make a delicate, feminine necklace.

You Will Need

Materials:

Sterling silver chain

24-gauge sterling silver wire (dead soft or half hard)

Swarovski Austrian crystals

2 split rings

Lobster claw or spring ring clasp

Tools:

Round-nose pliers

Chain-nose pliers

Wire cutters

▦ MAKING THE NECKLACE ▦

1 Find the center of the sterling silver chain.

2 Cut a three-inch piece of silver wire. Rest the wire on your forefinger. Using the round-nose pliers, bend one end upward about ½ inch from the end, forming a 45-degree angle.

3 Slide a crystal teardrop onto the long part of the bent wire and bend the wire on the other side of the crystal so that a triangle is created above the crystal.

4 With one hand, place the chain-nose pliers where the wire intersects in an "x" at the top of the triangle. Using the round-nose pliers in your other hand, wrap the shorter side of wire around the longer side three times. Clip off the excess wire off. Using your chain-nose pliers, tuck the cut part so it's flush and not sticking out. (See photo A.)

5 String two matching bicone crystals with spacer beads onto the wire. (See photo B.)

6 Place your round-nose pliers ⅓ inch above the crystals and bend the wire into a loop.

7 Slip the tail of the loop through the middle link of the sterling silver chain.

8 Wrap the loop tail around the wire three times. Snip and tuck the wire as you did in step 4.

9 Cut a 2-inch length of silver wire and create a loop about 1 inch from the end.

10 String the tail of this loop through the last link

of the chain and wrap the wire three times as above.

11 String two matching crystals with spacer beads onto the wire, then make the same loop on the other side.

12 Thread the tail of this loop through a clasp (lobster claw or spring ring) and wrap three times, then cut and tuck as above.

13 Repeat this process on the other end of the necklace and attach a split ring for the clasp to hook onto.

14 Optional: Add an antique look to the necklace by oxidizing it with a commercial solution (carefully following the manufacturer's directions and safety precautions) or with the natural technique on page 25. Note: Additional wire-wrapped spacers can be inserted for a more decorative look.

TIPS | DIY Network Crafts

Easy Matching Earrings

As you wrapped the teardrop that hangs from the necklace's chain, you probably realized what a glamorous earring it would make! To make earrings, make two more drops and slip the final tail of each loop (step 7) through the loop of an ear wire. Wrap the loop tail, snip, and tuck away the end to finish.

Designer: **Kelli Zusho**

VELVET PEARL PENDANT & LAYERED NECKLACE

This pearl trapeze pendant can be worn alone or with a matching opera-length pearl necklace to create the popular "layered look."

You Will Need

Materials:

- 87" length of velvet cord
- 2 6mm silver rondelle beads
- 3 3mm silver round beads
- 9" length of small, oval-link chain
- 10" sterling silver wire
- 4 10mm oval shaped freshwater pearls
- 1" headpin

Tools:

- 2 pairs round-nose pliers
- Wire cutters
- Scissors
- 3" piece of beading wire for a needle

MAKING THE NECKLACE

1 Cut three 29-inch lengths of velvet cord and set them aside.

2 Cut 12 ¾-inch lengths of chain.

3 Cut three 2-inch lengths of wire and one 3½-inch length of wire.

4 Lay out the pattern with the loose wire, beads, and chain.

TIPS | DIY Network Crafts

Getting the Right Look

The key to successful layering is to repeat at least one element that will pull it together. Mix up gold and silver, or heavy and light chain, but use garnets and pearls in every layer. You get the idea!

5 Build each element of the pendant by progressing from top to bottom and from left to right. (See diagram.)

6 Use a 2-inch piece of wire to create a wire-wrapped bead that connects to one large silver rondelle to form the pendant top. (This wire-wrapping technique is explained in the Crystal Pearl Bracelet on page 81.)

7 String a silver bead on the wire, then wire-wrap chains A and B together.

8 At the opposite end of chain A, use another 2-inch piece of wire to wrap chains A, C, and D together. String them on the wire in that order, forming the loop downward. When the wrap is complete, chain A should be on the top side of the loop and chains C and D should be on the bottom side of the loop ready to form the next triangle.

Continued on page 80.

OPERA-LENGTH NECKLACE

MAKING THE NECKLACE

1 Cut four 4½-inch lengths of chain.

2 Cut four 12-inch lengths of the beading wire.

3 Attach a length of beading wire to a length of chain with a crimp bead.

4 Alternate threading the silver and crystal beads five times, insert a crystal rondelle, and repeat until there are 9 inches of beaded wire.

5 Attach the strand from step 4 to another piece of chain with a crimp bead.

6 Attach another piece of beading wire to other end of chain. Thread on a four-bead pattern of a silver bead, an oval pearl bead, another silver bead, then a diamond-shaped pearl. Repeat for 9 inches, then attach it to the next piece of chain.

7 Repeat steps 3-6 two more times until the strand equals 54 inches.

8 Attach the clasp and extender chain.

9 Use the headpin and wire-wrap a crystal dangle from the last link of the extender chain.

You Will Need

Materials:

18" chain
56" length of beading wire
Strand of 3mm silver beads
Strand of 10mm oval-shaped, faceted freshwater pearls
Strand diamond-shaped freshwater pearls
Strand 6mm white opal crystals
10 6mm aurora borealis crystal rondelles
Silver crimp beads
Fancy hook clasp
1' length of extender chain

9 Thread a pearl onto the wire, then wire-wrap chains E, F, and B together.

10 At the opposite end of chain C, use the 3½-inch piece of wire to wrap chains C and G together.

11 String the following materials onto the wire in this order: a pearl, chain H, the opposite end of chain D, a silver bead, the opposite end of chain E, chain I, another pearl. Wrap chain J and chain F to the end.

12 Use a 2-inch piece of wire to wrap opposite ends of chains H and G and chain K together. String them on the wire in that order, as in step 9.

13 String a pearl on the wire, then wire wrap chains I, J and L together in that order).

14 Thread a headpin and a small silver bead, then wire-wrap them to the opposite ends of chains K and L.

15 Use the beading wire to create a loop and run the three ends of velvet cord through the loop. Thread the beading wire and the velvet cord through the large silver rondelle so that the pendant hangs from the center of the cords.

16 Thread all six ends of velvet through another rondelle for a sliding clasp. Knot all of the velvet ends to secure the necklace. The necklace is long enough to fit over your head, and the rondelle near the knot can be adjusted to shorten the necklace.

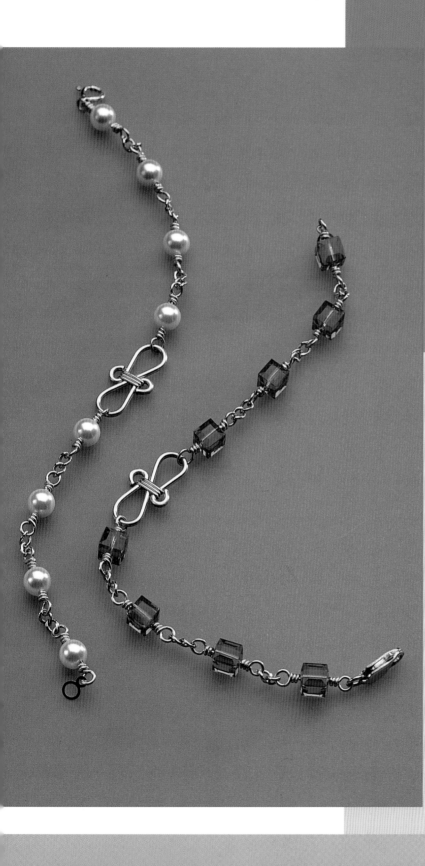

diy network

◀ Designer: **Gary Helwig** ▶

CRYSTAL PEARL BRACELET

These bead and wire bracelets are simple to make and fun to mix and match. Make extra wire links and use them in earrings and necklaces.

You Will Need

Materials:

4" length of 18-gauge wire*

30" length of 22-gauge wire

4" length of 24-gauge wire (optional)

8 6mm beads (crystals or pearls)

Clasp

6" length of medium or fine chain

*Any wire will do, but half-hard wire works best because it will require less hardening when the wire component is complete.

Tools:

Round-nose pliers

Bent chain-nose pliers

Flush cutter

Small jig with 2 small pegs and 2 large pegs (³⁄₁₆" recommended)

Chasing hammer and anvil (optional)

Nylon jaw pliers (optional)

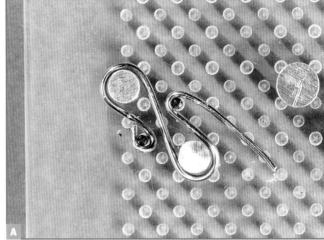

MAKING THE BRACELET

1 Straighten the 18-gauge wire. Using round-nose pliers, make a loop large enough to fit over the small metal pegs on the jig on one end of the wire.

2 Position two metal pegs and two large pegs in the jig. (See photo A.)

3 Place the initial loop in the 18-gauge wire on one of the small metal pegs in the jig and wrap the wire as shown. Push the wire down while wrapping, holding the wire straight.

4 Remove the wire from the jig and cut the excess wire tail with flush cutters. (See photo B.)

5 Close the final loop with bent chain-nose pliers. At this point the piece can be used as is, or, optionally (and recommended), it can be hardened by hammering it on an anvil with a chasing hammer. (See photo C.) A final option is to wrap 24-gauge wire around the middle of the piece to further strengthen it. The unit you've just finished is called a Flemish Spiral and is the centerpiece of the bracelet. The bracelet is built out from the center.

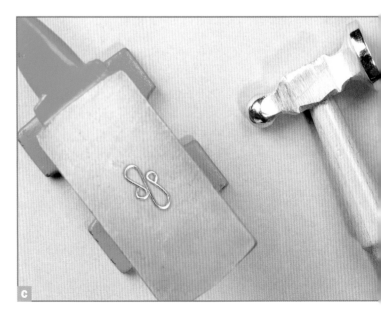

6 Cut six pieces of chain approximately ⅜ inches each.

7 Using the 22-gauge wire and a 6mm bead, make a wrapped bead link on one end of the Flemish Spiral. Connect the initial end of the wrapped bead link around one end of the Flemish Spiral and wrap that end closed. Add the 6mm bead and begin making the other end of the wrapped bead link. Before wrapping the other end of the wrapped bead link closed, connect it to the end link on one piece of chain. Once the chain has been added, complete the wrapped bead link by wrapping it closed.

8 Make two more wrapped bead links between the end of the chain and two more pieces of chain.

9 Make a fourth wrapped bead link between the end of the last piece of chain and half of the clasp.

10 Repeat steps 7 through 9 on the other end of the Flemish Spiral to make the other half of the bracelet.

TIPS | DIY Network Crafts

Strengthening the Wire

For durability, it's important to take the time to temper, or harden, the wrapped wire. Metal gets harder as it's used — the molecules strengthen their bond to each other. By hammering the wire loops and coils after they are made with a smooth leather or nylon hammer, you'll strengthen the wire and help it hold its shape.

FLEMISH SPIRAL EARRINGS

You Will Need

Materials:

Pair of earring posts with loops
8" length of 22-gauge wire
6 2" headpins
4 6mm beads
2 8-10mm beads

MAKING THE EARRINGS

1 Make two Flemish Spirals as directed in steps 1 through 5 for the bracelet. Wrap 4 inches of 22-gauge wire three times around the "waist" area through the two small loops. Trim the excess wire at the back.

2 For each earring, take a headpin, thread it through one of the 6mm beads, make a loop and wrap to make a dangle. Attach this to one side of the Flemish Spiral. Make a second dangle to attach to the other side. Then make a third dangle with one of the larger beads for hanging at the bottom of the Flemish Spiral.

3 Open the loops on the earrings and attach the Flemish Spirals.

Variation

■ Designer: **Kelli Zusho** ■

BLACK & WHITE NECKLACE

Knotted black velvet becomes part of the design in this modern necklace, creating a chic, urban look.

You Will Need

Materials:

3' 24-gauge sterling silver half-hard wire
4 onyx rondelles
14 arched silver tubes
32 3mm diamond cut silver beads
Onyx teardrop
Glue
1 9mm trigger clasp
20" velvet cord
3" oval silver extension chain
4 1" ball-tipped headpins
6mm silver rondelle
2 split rings
3 daisy spacer beads

Tools:

2 pairs round-nose pliers
Wire cutters
Scissors

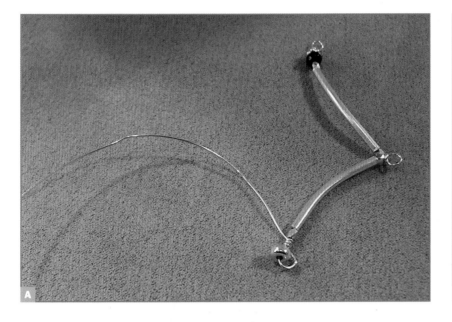

MAKING THE NECKLACE

1 Cut a 9-inch length of wire and slide the silver rondelle to the middle. Twist twice to secure the rondelle, which will be the bail of the pendant.

2 Form the wire into an arc shape. Thread a diamond-cut bead, a tube, another diamond-cut bead onto the wire. Form a loop in the wire with two twists. (See photo A.)

3 Repeat step 2 until second loop.

4 Repeat the process for other side and finish it by twisting the two wires together twice. Trim away one piece of wire and add an onyx rondelle. Wire- wrap a loop with the remaining wire.

5 Cut a 20-inch length of velvet cord. Knot one end, then knot again over the first knot. Thread the end cap, crimp it shut, and double knot again. Dab a dot of glue on the end of each knot.

6 String a diamond-cut bead, an arched tube, and another diamond-cut bead, then double knot.

7 Repeat step 6 four times and double knot. Add the pendant and double knot again.

8 Repeat steps 6 and 7 for the other half of necklace.

9 Attach a split ring to each of the end caps, adding the clasp to one end and the extension chain to the other. (See photo B.)

10 Thread a daisy spacer and an onyx rondelle (one each) onto a headpin. Wire-wrap to the end of the extension chain and repeat to hang dangles from the two sides of the pendant.

11 Wire-wrap the onyx briolette and add a diamond-cut bead. Wire-wrap it to dangle from the bottom of pendant.

TIPS DIY Network Crafts

Choosing the Right Cord
To avoid frustration, purchase the finest cord you can find. Bring it with you when you shop for beads so you can be sure the beads fit over the cord.

◀ Designer: **Jackie Guerra** ▶

BOHO HAND WRAP

You'll feel exotic when you wear this sparkling hand wrap. For fun variations, oxidize the silver for more impact or add a chain extension to make a choker.

You Will Need

Materials

- 17 11mm Austrian crystal rosettes with 3 loops
- 44 4mm Austrian bicone crystals to match
- 6x11mm Austrian crystal briolette
- 5x10mm silver lobster clasp
- 5" silver chain
- 2 3mm silver open jump rings
- 70" 24-gauge sterling silver half-hard wire
- 2 silver headpins
- Oxidizing solution

Tools:

- Round-nose pliers
- Flat-nose pliers
- Flush-wire cutters

MAKING THE WRAP

1 Cut 44 pieces of silver wire to 1½-inch lengths. (Silver eyepins the same length can be substituted when wire-wrapping the crystals.)

2 Place all the silver into the oxidizing solution. (See basic instructions on page 25.)

3 Arrange the rosettes on a flat surface with eight in the top row, five in the second row, four in the third row, and one in the last row. Alternate the directions of the rosettes in the top row so that the "triangles" of the three loops rotate — two on top, one on top, etc, across the row — so the the rest of the bracelet will drape beautifully on the hand.

4 Attach the top row of rosettes across the top and the bottom with a wire-wrapped crystal between each rosette

5 For the second row, attach the wire-wrapped crystals to the top two loops of each rosette and space them across, attaching them to the loops on the rosettes above.

6 For the third row, repeat with four rosettes with their two loops on the top. Attach wire-wrapped crystals to each of the top loops and connect them to the bottom loops of the second row.

7 Attach the last rosette with wire-wrapped crystals to the center two rosettes in the third row.

8 Using the headpins, dangle a crystal from the bottom loop of the two end rosettes in the second row.

9 Attach a wire-wrapped crystal from the bottom of the rosette in the fourth row.

10 With a longer piece of wire, wrap a hanger for the briolette. Create a loop at the top large enough to fit into the bottom loop of the wire-wrapped crystal in step 9, and two more wire-wrapped crystals (to be formed in step 11).

11 Cut a 3-inch length of chain, and attach two wire-wrapped crystals to each end. Attach the two ends of the chain and crystals to the top loop of the hanging briolette. This loop of wire will fit over a finger to hold the hand wrap in place.

12 Attach the lobster clasp to the last loop on the top row of rosettes on one side. On the other side, attach the remaining chain to the loop of the rosette with one last wire-wrapped crystal. Install the jump ring on the end of the chain.

TIPS | DIY Network Crafts

A One-Handed Clasp

When you're going to have to put a bracelet like this on yourself, pick a clasp that's easy to manipulate with one hand. A lobster clasp works well. Test it before buying!

4

Knitting, Crochet, & Knotting

Sew, you wanna make some jewelry? If you have yarn or thread, and you have beads, why not crochet them? Or knit them? Or knot them? Of course! What's more classic than a simple pearl necklace with a knot between each pearl? And what if those knots become part of the design, as they do in macramé? How about simply sewing beads onto a framework? If you already know how to knit or crochet, you're halfway there. If you don't, it's amazingly easy to learn the basic steps and start making one-of-a-kind jewelry pieces.

◄ Designer: **Cathi Milligan** ►

MODERN MACRAMÉ NECKLACE

Whether you're a flower child in hiding or just love '60's fashion, this classic macramé necklace is for you.

You Will Need

Materials

Centerpiece donut bead

Accent beads

Waxed linen cord

Hook clasp and jump ring

Macramé board or cardboard

T-pins

Tools

Tape

Glue

Toothpicks

KNOTTING THE MACRAMÉ NECKLACE

1 Choose a centerpiece donut bead large enough to accommodate several strands of waxed linen cord.

2 Cut four strands of waxed cord four to six times the length you'd like your finished necklace. It's better to have too much cord than not enough.

3 To form a Lark's Head knot, first fold a strand of cord in half. Take the loop end and thread it through the opening in your

donut bead, then pass the other end through the loop and tighten. This step creates two strands of cord for each original piece of cord. (See page 16.)

4 Repeat step 3 with the remaining three cords for a total of eight strands. You will work four strands on each side, one side at a time.

5 Tie the cords on one side (four strands) up in a bobbin so they don't get in the way while you work the other side.

6 Anchor the centerpiece down to the macramé board with a t-pin.

7 Start with a square knot. Separate the four cords so they lie flat. The two center cords are the holding cords and the outside two are the knotting cords. Tape down the center two cords and begin your first knot with the outer two cords. Make two half-knots, one to the left and one to the right, by looping the cord through the holding cords. Make sure that the second knot is tight. (See page 16.)

8 Remove the tape on the holding cords and thread an accent bead on. Repeat another square knot to secure the bead as in the previous step. (See photo A.)

9 Leave a bit of space in the cord before starting the next knotting sequence, which will be half-knot twists. Half-knot twists are made by continuing the half-knot in the same direction. (See page 16.) Make a half-knot, left to right, then another, left to right, to create a twist. At least 6 knots are needed to get the spiral to form. (See photo B.)

10 Leaving a little space, repeat the sequences in steps 7-9, starting with square knots, then adding an accent bead, a square knot, and then the half-knot twists.

11 When you have reached your desired length, repeat the entire process on the other side of the centerpiece bead.

12 Tie each set of cords onto the jump ring and hook clasp using an overhand knot, tying as tight as possible.

13 Apply a dab of glue on the knot with a toothpick. After the glue dries, trim cords close to the knot.

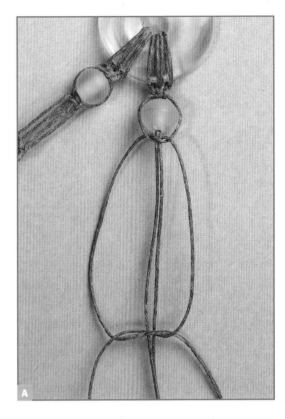

Designer: **Marilyn Johnson**

KNOTTED BOHEMIAN TREASURE NECKLACE

This project is a great way to use some of that leftover yarn, cord, and ribbon — just add big beads and charms. It's made with the easiest knot of all, the golden overhand.

You Will Need

Materials

- 2½ to 3 yards satin cord in main color
- 2½ to 3 yards twisted cord in contrasting or complementary color
- 2½ to 3 yards satin cord in contrasting or complementary color
- 2½ to 3 yards sheer ribbon in main color
- 4 yards narrow ribbon in main color
- 4 yards narrow ribbon in contrasting or complementary color
- 4 yards 2-ply waxed linen, any color
- Size 8 Perle cotton in contrasting or complementary color
- Pendant or focal bead with large hole or jump ring
- 20 to 30 assorted charms
- 25 3mm beads
- 25 4mm beads
- 20 6mm beads
- 20 to 25 8 or 10 mm beads
- 40 grams "E" beads, 20 in main color and 20 in contrasting or complementary color
- Size 8 seed beads
- Size 11 seed beads
- Decorative button or toggle clasp

Tools

- Scissors
- Dental floss threaders
- Cement glue
- Awl

MAKING THE NECKLACE

1 Assemble all stringing material — cord, ribbon, linen, and cotton — into one unit. The materials should be even with each other at the top end; the waxed linen and perle cotton will be longer than the other materials. Fold the material in half so that you can see the center.

2 String on a pendant or focal bead, making sure the pendant loop or bead hole is large enough for all stringing material to fit through.

3 If you're using a pendant, tie an overhand knot over the loop and pull it tight. If you're using a bead, tie an overhand knot along each side of the bead. (See figure below.)

Overhand Knot

4 To make the fringe, thread a piece of the waxed linen or pearl cotton through a dental floss threader and string on five to eight seed beads (depending upon length of fringe desired) and a charm.

5 Bring threader back through the last seed bead, working it up through all previous beads and tie onto the cords.

6 On the main necklace, thread on another bead which will lie flat; tie another overhand knot on the side of this bead, using whichever strands of thread that will fit through the hole of this bead.

7 Continue adding fringe and beads, knotting after each bit is added.

8 To end one side, twist all pieces of stringing material together except for pearl cotton and waxed linen. Wind the pearl cotton and waxed linen (waxed linen is "waxy" enough to aid in securing stringing materials) around the twisted materials until all have been covered. Form a loop and use the waxed linen to wrap around the base of the loop. Using a threaded needle, weave the waxed linen in and out of the covering, tie a knot, and wrap and weave in and out again. Tie a knot, then secure with glue.

9 Position a decorative button on the opposite side, then tie a knot on both sides of the button. Repeat the twisting and wrapping process from step 8 for just long enough to create room to form a small loop to fit under the button, forming its base.

10 Glue the ends of the knots for the both the button and the loop ends.

11 Cut leftover stringing material after glue has dried.

◀ Designer: **Jill Atkins** ▶

BEAD GOULASH BRACELET

Anything goes when selecting beads for this bracelet —anything! Mix and match your orphan beads, mixing them up to make a charming, eclectic bracelet.

You Will Need

Materials:

- #2 rattail cord
- Focal bead, optional
- Bead assortment in different sizes, shapes, and textures

Tools:

- Glue to prevent fraying
- Nylon beading thread, size "B"
- Size 10 beading needle

MAKING THE BRACELET

1. Cut two pieces of rattail, one 32 inches in length and the second 16 inches. Loop the long piece at the top and insert the short piece in between.

2. Sew several stitches an inch down from the loop's end to secure the three strands together.

3. Braid the three strands all the way to the end and tie a knot in end. (See photo A.)

4. To check the length, wrap the braid around your wrist, adjusting the position of the knot as needed. (The knot will become the "button" that slips through the loop at the top.) Sew some stabilizing stitches through the knot so it won't come undone.

5. Cut away the excess cord at the knot end and the loose end at the top inside the loop. Dot with glue to prevent fraying.

6. Sew the focal bead onto the knot. Decorate the rest of the knot by sewing some of your "bead goulash" all over it.

7. Sew small beads around the loop at the top, making sure the loop still fits over the knot. (See photo B.)

8. Decorate the rest of the bracelet by sewing beads and creating fringes, clustering extra beads at the center of the bracelet and on either side. and on either side.

A

B

Designer: **Lily Chin**

KNITTED CHOKER

For a great vintage look with seed beads, try knitting! Only the most basic stitches — and some beautiful beads — are required.

You Will Need

Materials

100 m of 100% mercerized cotton or silk thread, size #10

Approximately 750 size 11 glass seed beads

Clasp

Tools:

Bead-stringing needle if beads are not strung onto thread

Double-pointed knitting needles (dpn), size 000 (1.5 mm)

Thin tapestry or beading needle

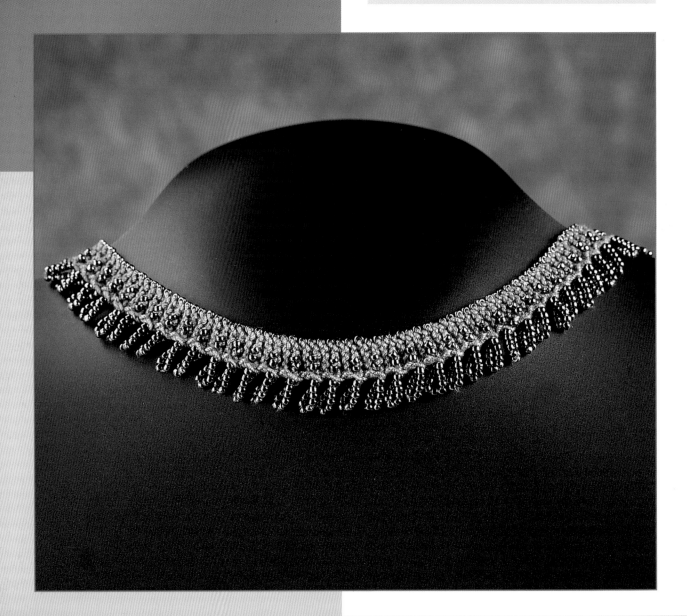

MAKING THE CHOKER

1 Pre-string the beads onto the knitting thread with bead-stringing needle.

2 Cast 4 stitches onto knitting needles, leaving a 4"-inch tail at beginning.

3 Work I-cord without beads for ½ inch. To work I-cord, k* across with another dpn. DO NOT TURN WORK and always have Right Side or k side facing you. Slide all sts to right-hand end of dpn. String strand of yarn across back of work and repeat from *. Tug on cord slightly lengthwise. (This cord is similar to that made by "knitting knobbies" and looks like small, circular tube.)

4 Increase 1 st in center stitch on last row–5 sts. Turn work.

5 Begin the knitting pattern as follows:
- **Row 1:** (Wrong Side) Bring Up Bead or BUB, knit 1 through back loop or tbl, [knit 1, BUB] twice, k 1, p 1.
- **Row 2:** (Right Side) BUB 11, k 1 tbl, knit 4.
- **Row 3:** BUB, k 1 tbl, k 4.
- **Row 4:** Slip1 stitch with yarn in front, bring yarn to back, knit 4.

6 Repeat Rows 1 through 4 for pattern until piece measures approximately 10½ inches or ½ inch less than the desired length. Stop after completing Row 2 of pattern.

7 Work the next row as follows: k2, k2 together, k1 (there are now 4 stitches).

8 Work I-cord without beads for ½ inch. Bind off all sts. Leave 4 inches of length of tail at end.

9 Steam block if desired.

10 Using yarn tails, sew half of the clasp to each end.

KNITTING ABBREVIATIONS USED

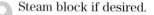

BUB	Bring Up Bead
dec	Decrease
dpn	Double-pointed needles
inc	Increase
k	knit
p	purl
st(s)	stitch(es)
tbl	through back loop
*	repeat

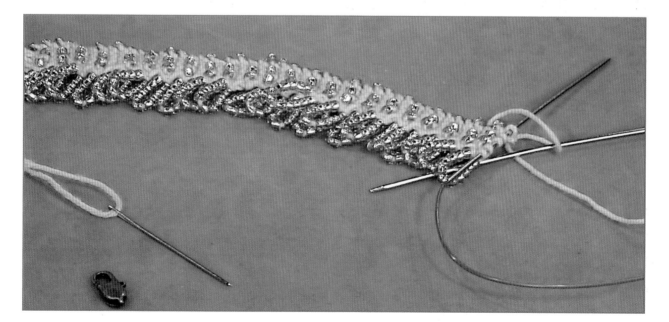

network

■ Designer: **Judy Hendrix** ►

BEADED CABOCHON

Here's a technique for creating an embellished framework around a centerpiece button or stone. Use the embellished framework as the focal point of a necklace, a bracelet, or a belt.

You Will Need

Materials	Tools:
Special button or cabochon gemstone	Extra-strong clear craft adhesive
3" square of fine suede	Size 10 sharp needle
3" square of felt	Size 10 beading needle
Size 11 seed beads	Craft scissors and small, sharp-point scissors
Nylon beading thread, size D	Bead tray

1 If you're using a button with a shank, remove the shank from the back of the button. Glue the button or cabochon to the three-inch piece of felt and let it dry overnight.

2 Thread the long beading needle with 36 inches of beading thread. Double it and secure with a triple knot. This thread and needle will be used to string the beads. Thread the short needle with a single 18-inch piece of thread; knot one end with a secure triple knot.

3 Coming up from the back side with the long needle, pull the thread through to the front, right next to the button. Begin "stringing" the first row of beads, enough to go approximately around the button. (Don't worry about having too many. Excess beads will be taken care of later.)

4 Move the stringing thread to the side of your workspace. Bring the single thread up from the back, next to the button and between the beads, at the third bead. The single strand will be used to couch the beads into place.

5 Cross the single thread over the double thread in between beads (about every third bead). Hold the threads tight against the previous bead, take a stitch over the double thread, keeping them as tight as possible to prevent gaps. ALWAYS come up next to the button (or the subsequent rows next to the completed row) and stitch out toward the edge. Continue couching all the way around until there is space left for the last two or three beads to complete the row.

6 Check the remaining space to be sure the last beads won't buckle or leave a gap, then drop the excess beads off of the double thread. Take the double thread with the last loose beads on it and go back through the first four beads that were couched (should be right in front of the loose beads). Take the single thread and couch these last loose beads to make a nice, finished look. Take both needles to the back. (You will always take both threads to the back before beginning a new row.)

7 Use a new bead color for the second row or mix and match. Remember to couch from near the button to

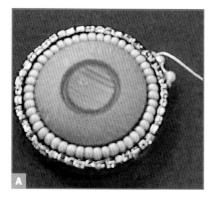

A

the outside. Bring threads to the back and knot securely. Repeat a third row in the same way. (See Photo A.)

8 Working from the back (so that the couching threads aren't clipped), trim the felt as close as possible to the beads. It's best if no felt can be seen when looking at the front. (If you're using a holed button, string beads from one hole to another before adding the back. Later, they can be embellished even more.)

9 Thread a beading needle with a single thread about 36 inches long. Knot the thread, then anchor it securely somewhere on the back. Come up anywhere on the front between two rows of beads. Leave the thread hanging from the front, to use later.

10 Glue a piece of ultrasuede to the back of the button. Trim the suede evenly, but not too short, since there needs to be room to stitch through it.

FINISHING

1 With your beading needle, take the thread you left hanging in the front. To position the needle, feed it under the outside row of

beading and exit between the felt and the suede. You want to be between the two layers.

2 This row is unique (it's embellished) and requires flipping the button from front to back to create an edging that is NOT measured against the couched beads. The spacing should be as even as possible. String three beads on the thread and measure over to the LEFT (for right-handed people) the width of one bead and take your needle straight through to the back.

3 Turn the whole button over (looking at the back now) and come up from the bottom, go through the last bead on the right. The thread and needle are coming out of the top of the bead so that they are in position for the next step.

4 Turn the button back to the front. Remember: on the front, stitch to the left; on the back, come up through the last bead on the right. Add two beads (on the left) now, go straight back through all the layers, turn the button over and come up in the last bead on the right. Continue all the way around, evenly spaced, until you have space for one more bead.

5 Turn the button to the back (only because it is easier to see) and add one bead. Take the needle down into the top of the first bead put on; it connects the row. Go to the left and come up in the bead next to that, to have your needle in position for finishing. (The next row is the embellished row, with two twisted rows of beads.)

6 Put the needle through one of the laying down beads, string four beads, skip a laying-down bead and go into the next laying down bead. Continue all the way around to create a scalloped edge. (See Photo B.)

B

7 With a contrasting bead, twist around the first row. Again, take the needle through a laying down bead that was skipped the first time around, add four beads, this time going over the top of the first row and taking the needle into the next skipped bead. It should look like it is twisting around the outer edge. (See photo C.) Knot off the thread on the back, then use the embellished cabochon in a project.

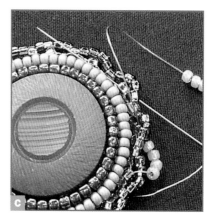

C

◄ Designer: **Akiko Masuda** ►

CROCHETED & BRAIDED NECKLACE

This necklace uses two simple "non-jewelry" techniques — crochet and common braiding — to make a beautiful necklace!

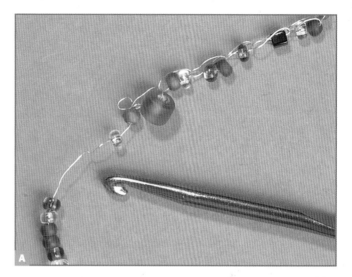

You Will Need

Materials

#28 gauge silver wire

Variety of colors, shapes, and sizes of Czech and Japanese glass beads

Variety of colors, shapes, and sizes of Austrian Crystal beads

Jump rings

Clasp

Tools:

Wire cutters

#8 Crochet hook

MAKING THE NECKLACE

1 Cut the silver wire into three 70-inch lengths. Randomly bead ⅓ of each length of wire with a variety of colors, shapes, and sizes of glass and crystal beads.

2 Using the crochet hook, begin crocheting each of the wires separately in a simple chain stitch, incorporating a bead in each stitch until all three wires are finished (See photos A and B.). Pull the wire out through the last loop to prevent unraveling.

3 Twist the three wires together at one end.

4 Braid the three crocheted strands together, then twist the ends of the wires together. (See Photo C.)

5 Lastly, add the jump ring and the clasp. Be sure all the ends of the wire are trimmed off and tucked away to prevent scratching.

◣ Designer: **Marilyn Johnson** ◢

CLASSIC KNOTTED NECKLACE

This project uses a classic knotting technique known for its ability to make a necklace flow around the wearer's neck. Kick it up a notch by using colored silk and clear gemstones that allow the silk to show through. The technique is simple; you just need a little practice to make perfect!

You Will Need

Materials	Tools:
French wire	Wire cutters
Gemstones or beads of your choice	Cement glue
2 packages of knotting silk with needle attached	Beading tweezers or beading awl
Clasp	Scissors

KNOTTING THE NECKLACE

1 Cut two pieces of French wire, one ¼ inch long and one ½ inch long. Set aside.

2 String three beads on to the silk with attached needle; bring the beads to the end of the silk, leaving a two-inch tail.

3 Gently guide on one piece of French wire, stopping at the last added bead. (See photo A.)

4 String the clasp through its loop.

5 Bring the needle through last bead added and tie an overhand knot. Use the tweezers or the awl to hold the end of the silk near the bead, then tighten the knot closest to the head.

6 Bring the needle through the next bead and tie a knot.

7 Repeat the process on the remaining bead. Tie the knot using the thread from the tail and thread from the needle.

8 Place just a bit of glue on the last knot and a bit of tail. (See photo B.)

A

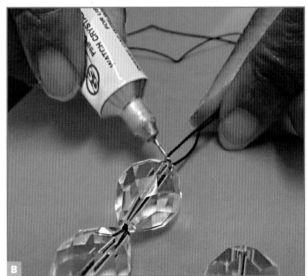

B

TIPS | DIY Network Crafts

Simple Clasp Attachment

A bead-tip clam shell clamp is an alternative way to attach the strand of knotted pearls or stones to the clasp without using French wire that many novices find easier to master. Run the silk through the hole, tie a firm double knot, add a drop of glue, and clamp the clam shell closed over the knot. When the glue is dry, trim away the extra silk. All that remains is to attach the loop of the clamp to the clasp and voilá!

9 Continue adding beads in this fashion until there are only three beads and French wire left.

10 Add the last three beads, leaving some leeway between the last three beads. Add the French wire and string on the clasp

11 Take the needle back through the last bead added and tie a knot.

12 Take the needle through the second to the last bead; knot and glue. When the glue is dry, cut thread tails.

diy network

◀ Designer: **Bethany Barry** ▶

BEAD CROCHET SPIRAL BRACELET

If you can crochet, you can make this bracelet. There are no hard and fast rules, just have fun making it!

You Will Need

Materials

- 8/0 seed beads in 4 matte colors (1 to 2 small tubes of each)
- Assorted accent beads (faceted beads, crystal cubes, polymer rondelles, glass butterflies, faceted beads, center beads, 6mm fiber optic beads, and others were used here)
- 2 pewter cones
- Magnetic clasp
- 69-weight upholstery thread

Gauge:

7 inches of strung beads will equal approximately 1½ inches of bead crochet, depending upon the tension.

Tools:

- Size 2 crochet hook
- Scissors
- Nail polish
- 2 1½" eye pins
- Round-nose pliers
- Chain-nose pliers
- Wire cutters
- Big-eye needle (optional)
- Anti-ravel stiffener (optional)

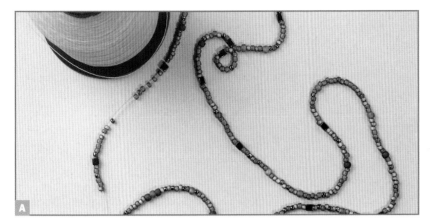

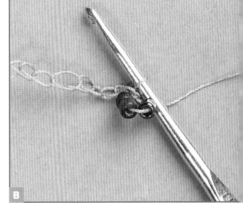

CROCHETING THE BRACELET

1 Mix all the 8/0 beads into a "bead soup." Check the color and balance, adjusting the balance if necessary.

2 Cut off the end of the thread at an angle, leaving it attached to the spool. Use it as is, or, to make life easier, use the big-eye needle or stiffen the thread with an anti-raveling agent.

3 Lay out the beads in a loose, pleasing design, such as a seven to eight 8/0 bead soup, a small accent bead, a seven to eight 8/0 bead soup, a crystal cube, seed beads, fiber optic beads, seed beads, etc., alternating shapes and sizes.

4 For a 7-inch bracelet (plus clasp), string approximately 49-55 inches of beads, ending with seed beads. Don't cut the thread! (See photo A.)

5 With the crochet hook, make a slip knot, leaving an 8-inch tail, and make a chain without beads measuring about 7¼ inches.

6 Work one row of single crochet without beads, and chain one stitch at the end of the row.

7 Begin a single crochet bead crochet, sliding up three seed beads at a time, another three seed beads, and another seed bead, an accent bead, and a seed bead, going into each stitch until the end of the row. Chain one stitch at the end. (See photo B.)

8 Work a row of single crochet without beads to the end, and chain one at the end.

9 Continue this pattern, alternating one row with beads and one row without beads to ensure the beads are only on one side — the side that will show! After a few rows of beads are crocheted, the work will begin to spiral. Allow the work to spiral, but try to keep the tension and balance consistent.

10 When the piece is as wide and spirally as desired (approximately six to eight rows; three with beads, four without), slipstitch the ends together into a circle to hold the spiral in its twisted position.

11 Work one to two rows of circular crochet, making a tiny tube that will fill the end of the cone.

12 Chain eight to ten stitches off the circle end, then stitch the last stitch back down into the circle end, making a loop to go through the end of the eyepin.

13 Open the eye of the eyepin with the round-nose pliers and place the crocheted loop into it. Close the eye snugly. Run the end of the eyepin through one of the cones, bend a loop on the end, and attach this loop onto the magnetic clasp.

14 Repeat the circular crochet in step 10, then continue with steps 11 and 12 to attach the cone and clasp to the other end of the bracelet.

diy network

5

Bead Weaving

Just like the projects in the Simple Stringing chapter, the jewelry showcased in this chapter is also made from string and beads. The unique structures in the finished pieces, though, look quite different than strung jewelry. A quick trip to a museum with ancient decorative arts shows us how many ways people throughout the ages have beautified their lives using weaving techniques. In fact, the names of the weaving techniques reflect their ethnic origins: "Peyote" weaving involves a frame with a warp and a weft; "Ndebele" weaving is done off-loom and creates a herringbone pattern by running the thread back through beads already threaded. Then, of course, there are embellishments and fringes that add beautiful touches to bead woven jewelry!

◄ Designer: **Sharon Bateman** ►

FRINGED AMULET BAG

Specialty tube bead weaving looms allow even beginners to have fun creating one-of-a-kind beaded bags.

You Will Need

Materials:

Hank of size 11/0 Czech seed beads in blue and one in translucent green

Size 'D' waxed nylon thread

Strand of pearls

Strand 4mm cobalt blue druks

Strand 4mm turquoise druks

Clasp of choice

Fabric glue

Tools:

Small tube loom

#12 beading needle

MAKING THE BAG

1 String 26 warp threads onto the loom following the manufacturer's instructions. Work the body of the bag using the blue seed beads. Sew the bottom of the bag closed.

2 Work a two-legged branch fringe (see sidebar on page 110) along the bottom of the bag. Follow the graph provided for bead placement and combination of techniques and beads.

3 Work a Mandala edging along the top edge of the bag. (See page 124 for instructions.)

Top Mandala Edging

4 Add a row of simple fringe along the front of bag. (See sidebar on page 110.)

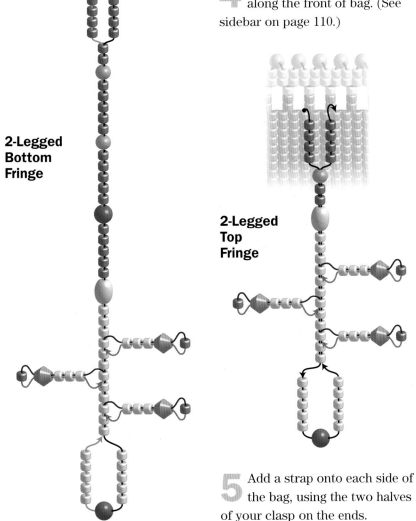

2-Legged Bottom Fringe

2-Legged Top Fringe

5 Add a strap onto each side of the bag, using the two halves of your clasp on the ends.

TIPS | DIY Network Crafts

It's a matter of tension. The secret to great fringe is the tension. To look good, most fringe should be tight enough to not leave a gap and loose enough to be soft and flowing.

MAKING THE CORD

1 Tie onto the edge warp thread with a half hitch or leave a tail for multiple needles.

2 Weave down through the width of the row and back up to begin your strap. This process will not disturb the bead alignment. When weaving through the whole row is not possible, distribute the weight of the bag over a few rows. Less stress on the threads will reduce the likelihood of the tension pulling beads out of alignment.

Attaching the Cord

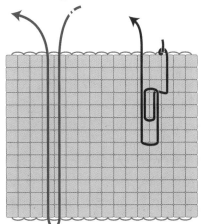

MAKING FRINGE

Simple Fringe

As with the edging, your fringe will be hooked onto your beadwork with a hook thread. Run in through beads, or run through layers of fabric. With your thread coming out of your beadwork, string on desired amount of beads for the fringe. Push the last bead aside and run back up through the beads just added. Pull all tight, and run back into the beadwork. Repeat along the edge.

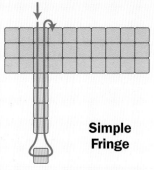

Simple Fringe

Two-Legged Fringe

With your thread coming out of your beadwork, string on desired amount of beads for the fringe. Push the last bead aside and run back up through the beads just added up to the beads assigned for the leg of the fringe. (Your fringe can be any length desired.) Pull all tight. String on the second leg of fringe, and run back into the beadwork a short space from the first leg. Repeat along the edge.

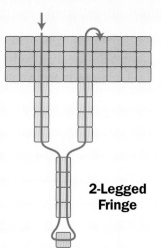

2-Legged Fringe

Branch Fringe

String on the length of the fringe. Push the last bead aside (stop bead) and run up a few beads. String on a branch, push aside the stop bead, and run back through the beads. Add branches in a random order, working in the same fashion all the way up the fringe.

For a stiff branch fringe, run back through the bead you come out of and keep the tension tight. For a loose grass fringe, you will run in between the beads and keep the tension loose. For a drooping branch fringe, work the grass technique with a heavy thread.

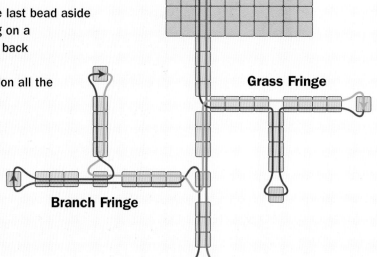

Grass Fringe

Branch Fringe

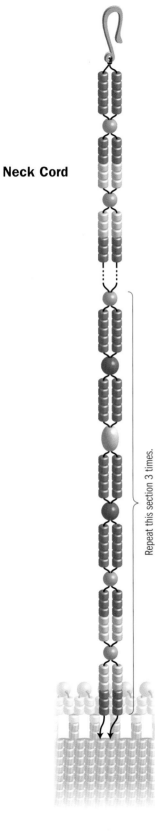

Neck Cord

Repeat this section 3 times.

3 Tie onto the edge and run down a row. Jump to the next row and run down a few beads. Square stitch on two rows. Run down a few beads, jump over a row and run up to the edge of the work.

MOUNTING THE CORD

1 With the loose end of your cord, tie a series of knots around the loop of the clasp. First knot: Run the end of the cord through the clasp ring. Bring the cord around and to the back of the ring and then through, in the opposite direction. Bring the end of the cord down through the loop that forms. This completes the lark's head knot, and secures the cord to the first half of the clasp.

2 Half hitch: Bring the end around the back and then across the front. Run the end through the loop that forms. Pull tight. This is a half hitch.

3 Repeat the half hitch five more times to form three double half hitches. Add a drop of fabric glue and rub into the fibers. Allow to completely dry. Check the end of the cord to make sure it's secure; if not, add glue again and allow to completely dry. Trim the end close.

Color Variation

◤ Designer: **Vicky Star** ◥

COMPUTER-DESIGNED FLOWER CUFF

Ndebele or herringbone weaving is an ancient technique that involves running the thread back and forth through beads that have already been strung to reinforce the finished piece. For best results, practice the directions for a few rows until you feel comfortable with the technique.

You Will Need

Materials:	Tools:
Japanese cylinder beads	Beading needle, size 10 or 11
Nylon beading thread, size B	Design image
Beeswax or other thread conditioner	Scissors
Hook-and-loop adhesive tape for clasp	Work surface or bead mat

⫸ PREPARING THE DESIGN ⫷

1 Transfer a color photo to graph paper so that the image fills a space 20 units wide by about 130 units long. Each square in the graph will represent a single color in your bracelet. (See sidebar.)

2 Select beads to match the colors on the graph, and set them out in a tray or on a mat.

3 Thread the beading needle with 3 yards of beading thread. Double the thread and run it across the beeswax, then run it twice through a stop bead, leaving a 6-inch tail.

⫸ ROWS 1 THROUGH 3 ⫷

1 Tie a stop bead 6 inches from the end of the thread with an overhand knot.

2 Thread beads for the first two rows onto the thread; in this case, 40 dark green beads.

3 String the third row as follows. Add first bead of row 3, turn, run the needle through the last bead, skip the next two, then run through the next one. Be sure that the needle doesn't split the thread as it runs through the beads.

4 Next, add two more beads, and run through the next one. (See photo on opposite page.)

5 Continue to the end of the row with this pattern: skip 2, through 1, add 2, through 1. As you go, pull on both tail and needle threads with even tension so that the beads "fold" into

place. These rows zigzag together and are three beads high.

ROWS 4 THROUGH 130

1 Add two beads, the last bead of current row and first bead of next row. Make a U turn and run through the last bead of the third row.

2 Work the herringbone stitch across (add 2 beads, through 2 beads). This stitch is like a roller coaster: go up to the peak, add two beads, and go down into the valley and cross to the next bead. Each row creates a new set of peaks, but the weave is reinforced through the valleys.

3 These are the pattern rows, and the work is turned over at the end of each row, so watch carefully to be sure you are adding in the colors correctly.

FINISHING

1 Work picots across ends: add 1 bead, through 2.

2 Sew on a small square of hook-and-loop adhesive tape on each end of the bracelet, positioning the squares so that when you wrap the bracelet around your wrist the pieces easily hold the ends of the bracelet together. Hide the stitches in the beads.

CREATING YOUR OWN DESIGN

Starting with a photograph or picture that you want to copy, it's possible to create a design on a grid, which is then used as a pattern for the project.

For a computer, it's necessary to have software designed to convert a digital or scanned picture into a graphic form.

Another method is to copy a colored photo onto graph paper at a copying store. Be sure that the photo will reproduce onto the graph paper in the right size so that you can correctly mark the shape of your project.

The "old-fashioned" technique still works: just use a ruler and pen to create a grid over the picture, making sure that the number of squares for the length and width will work for the project.

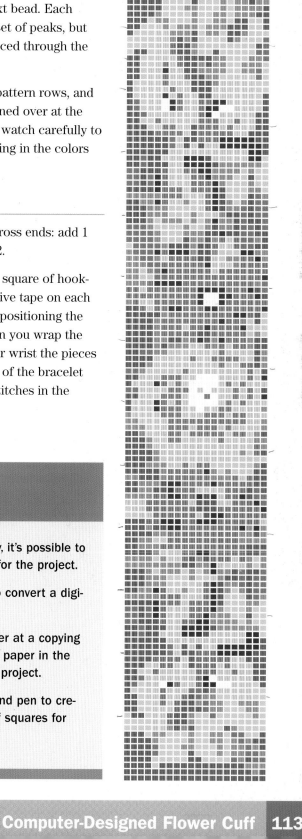

◀ Designer: **Sharon Bateman** ▶

FRILLY RING

There's no limit to what you can do with thread and beads and basic weaving techniques. You can even make this wild and crazy ring!

You Will Need

Materials:

Small amount of seed beads in one to three colors

Large 12-15 MM bead

Size D nylon beading thread

Tools:

#12 beading needle

*Note: Refer to the graphs for color placement.

▥▥ RING BASE ▥▥

A

1 Thread a needle with approximately 1½ yards of thread. Slipstitch a stop bead onto the end of the thread. String on 40 seed beads in the band color. Run through the last four and pull tight to form a circle. (See photo A.)

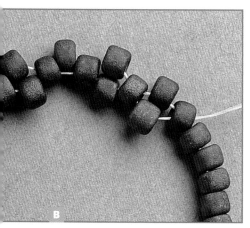

2 Peyote stitch around the beads you've just strung to form the first three rows of the band. Be sure to keep track of the step up to keep the bead count of each row even. (See photo B.)

3 Work four more rows for a total of seven rows. Keep working the step up by running through the first bead of each row to keep the count even.

THE ROOSTER TAILS

1 Refer to the diagram to review how the three rooster tail fringes are separated by a single peyote stitched bead on each side of the band.

Beading the Rooster Tail Fringe

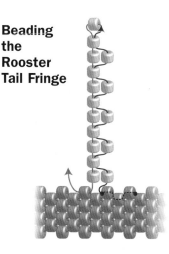

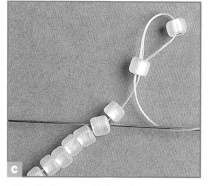

2 String on 11 beads. Push the last one aside and run through the second to form a stop bead. (See photo C.)

3 Peyote stitch down the fringe and run through the next stand up bead of the band. (See photo D.)

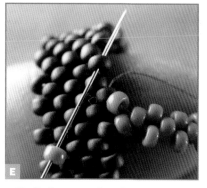

4 String on a bead and peyote stitch it to the next stand up bead. This is the bead that will separate the fringe. (See photo E.)

5 Work three rooster tails along one side. (See photo F.)

6 Run the needle through the beads to bring needle out to the opposite side. (See photo G.)

7 Work three rooster tails on the opposite side like the first three. (See photo H.)

CENTER BEADS

1 Run through three of the beads of the band coming out slightly off center and lined up between the first and second rooster tail on one side. (See photo I.)

2 String on five seed beads, the large MM bead and five more seed beads. (See photo J.)

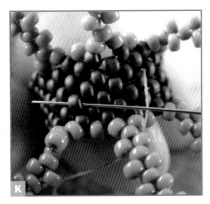

3 Run through a bead on the opposite side of band near the first and second rooster tail. (See photo K.)

4 Run the needle up through three of the last five seed beads strung on and pull tight. (See photo L.)

SETTING: ROW 1

1 (*) String on one seed bead and run up through the first

Beading Row 1

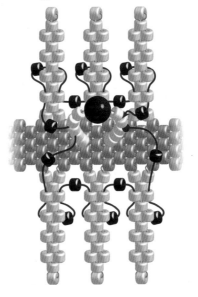

free standup bead of the nearest rooster tail. (See photo M.)

2 String on one seed bead and run down through the stand up bead on the opposite side of the rooster tail. (See photo N.)

3 Repeat from (*) across all three-rooster tails on this side. (See photo O.)

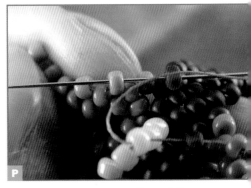

4 String on one seed bead. Run through the third bead on the leg of the center bead set. (See photo P.)

5 Work the seed beads along the next three rooster tails as in the first three. Pull the work tight so there are no gaps and the rooster tails stand up straight. (See photo Q.)

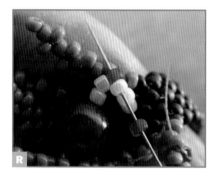

6 At the end of the row, run through the very first bead like any other stand up bead in a peyote stitch. (See photo R.)

SETTING: ROW 2

1 Work a row of peyote all around, remembering the stand up set (See photo S.)

Beading Row 2

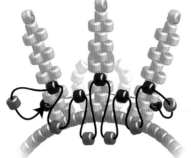

2 When the row is finished, pull it all tight so there are no gaps. (See photo T.)

SETTING: LAST ROW

1 String on three beads and run through the next stand up bead of the row. Run through the stop bead of the nearest rooster tail and run through the next stand up bead. (See photo U.)

2 Pull the thread tight so the rooster tail bends over and tucks into the peyote stitched row.

Work the next two rooster tails in the same fashion. (See photo V.)

3 Work an extra three-bead set onto the next bead and then begin alternating between adding three beads and stitching down the rooster tails. (See photo W.)

4 End the row by adding in an extra three-bead set and then running your needle through the next few beads. Tug everything tight and make sure it is all in order then tie off your thread. (See photo X.)

◢ Designer: **Sharon Bateman** ◣

PEYOTE SNAKE RING

Snakes don't have to be scary. Wrap this one around your finger and enjoy the attention!

⁝⁞⁞ MAKING THE RING ⁞⁞⁝

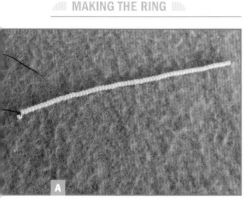

1 Thread the needle and tie one 14/0 bead onto the end of the thread. String on 68-14/0 beads. (See photo A.)

2 Run through the third bead from the end and pull tight so the last two beads are lying side by side. Begin the peyote stitch to create the rows using the 14/0 beads. (See photos B and C.)

3 Work three more rows for a total of six rows. (See photo D.)

4 Work 1 row of 11/0 beads. When you reach the end of the row, run through the beads along the end of the bead strip to the opposite side. (See photo E.)

5 Begin working the 11/0 beads onto this side of the strip. Once the 11/0 beads are worked onto both sides of the bead strip, it will begin to curl up a bit. (See photo F.)

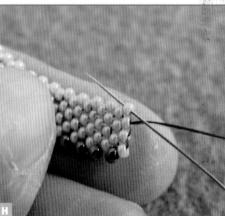

6 Use peyote stitch to sew the two 11/0 rows together. (They should fit together like the teeth of a zipper.) Run through these beads without adding any more. The result will be a beaded tube that spirals around. (See photos G and H.)

Once the bead strip is completed, work the tail thread left on the tied bead into the work; neatly tie off.

1 String on three beads in the body color, one bead in the stripe color, one in the body color, one bead in the stripe color, one in the body color, one in the stripe color, one in the body color, and three in the body color.

2 Push the last bead aside to form a stop bead and run through all but the last three beads.

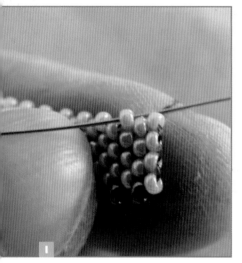

3 String on three beads in the body color and run down into the nearest bead of the bead strip. You've created two legs for the tail. (See photo I.)

4 Bring the needle up, add three beads in the body color, run all the way up to the stop bead, through it, and then back down.

Beading the Snake Tail

5 Add three final beads in the body color and work the thread into the beadwork; tie it off. (See photo J.)

1 Tie the thread onto the opposite end of the beaded tube, making sure it comes out of the beads at the end of the stripe where you will want the head of the snake.

2 Row 1: String on five beads and run back down through the closest bead on the beaded tube. (See photo K.)

Beading the Snake Head

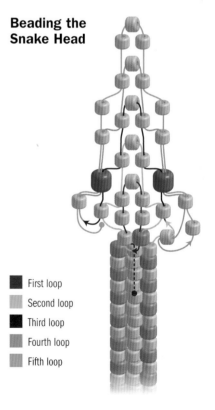

■ First loop
▨ Second loop
■ Third loop
▨ Fourth loop
▨ Fifth loop

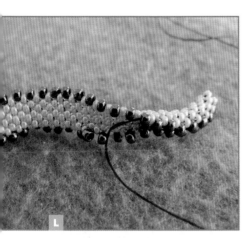

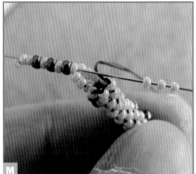

3 Row 2: Run up through the next bead along the end of the tube. String on one bead and run through the second bead (peyote stitch). (See photo L.) String on three beads and stitch onto the second bead away. (See photo M.) Work one more bead onto the first row of the head. (See photo N.)

4 Row 3: This row will make the eyes. Following the graph, and string on one 8/0 bead and run through the next bead of the first row. String on three 14/0 beads and run through the next bead. String on the second 8/0 bead and run through the next bead.

5 Row 4: Peyote stitch 14/0 beads along the row. Work the 8/0 beads just like the others and keep using the three beads at the tip to form the nose.

6 Row 5: String on a bead and run the needle through the 8/0 bead and the 14/0 beads before and after it. Work peyote on the rest of the row using the three-bead set at the tip. (See photo O.) Work the second eye like the first, by running through the three beads. (See photo P.)

FINISHING

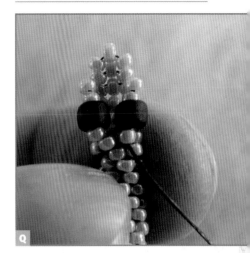

1 Your snake now has a flat head shape, like a cobra. For a sleeker, garden snake look, sew the jaws together. (See photo Q.)

2 Wrap the snake around a finger as it is, and it will fit any size finger. To size it permanently, wrap the snake around a ring mandrel and stitch it in place by sewing the head or tail to the point where it touches the body.

TIPS | DIY Network Crafts

Children Want Snakes, Too!

Once you start wearing your favorite snake rings, you'll have no shortage of young admirers. Make extras rings for the children in your life and string them alone or in groups on bright, colorful shoelace cords.

◀ Designer: **Sharon Bateman** ▶

LOOMED BRACELET

Once the loom is set up, this project is really easy. Soon you'll be creating your own loomed designs!

You Will Need

Materials

Bobbin of strong nylon thread, Size D, that complements color 1 (green)

½ tube each of two colors size 11 Japanese seed beads

42 4mm bicone crystals that match color 1

16 faceted fire polish crystals that match color 2 (copper)

16mm bead for clasp.

Tools:

Beading loom

#12 beading needle

MAKING THE BRACELET

1 Thread the loom using instructions provided by the loom's manufacturer. String on ten warp threads for the nine-bead width of the pattern. On any loom, the warp threads are strung lengthwise to provide support when the beads are woven to create the fabric of your work. When using a traditional loom, stretch 10 warp threads the length of your bracelet, plus 24 inches so you will have ample thread to weave the warp threads into the beadwork. It may be necessary to adapt the pattern depending on the size, length, and clasp desired. For the length of the bracelet, measure the length desired and make only the number of diamond motifs that will fit completely into the length. These instructions are for the diamond pattern.

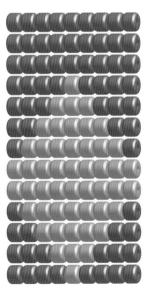

2 Weft threads are the threads that will hold the beads onto the warp threads. Thread the needle with a weft thread that is a comfortable length. Tie one end to the outside warp thread using a half hitch or overhand knot. String on the nine seed beads.

3 The next step is to weave the loom stitch. Place the weft thread with the first 9 beads under the warp threads to the opposite side. The warp threads will create a "parking place" for each bead. Push the beads up into those parking places and run the weft thread needle back in the other direction, through the beads, making sure it is over each of the warp threads as you work.

4 Work the rows following the graph. Color 1 is the base. Color 2 is the diamond shape. Repeat the Diamond Motif until there is no room left to work a complete one and fill in the remaining space with color 1 and tie off the weft thread with a few half hitches. Weave the tail into the beadwork for a few rows.

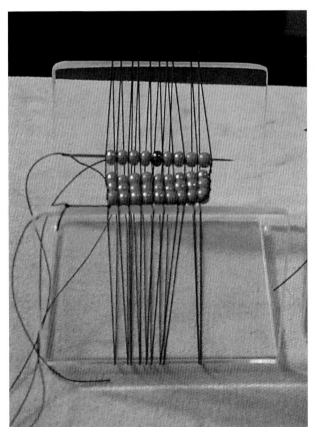

5 Remove the bracelet from the loom and rub it between your hands so that all the rows are spaced evenly.

6 To embellish the edge of the bracelet, work a Mandala edging of three bead picots (set of beads in the edging) along the section that is solid color 1, from one diamond point to the next. The sidebar shows the pattern for this edging and provides directions.

7 To add a loop and bead clasp when the edging is complete, first decide how far apart to place the button or bead and the loop clasp. Sew the button or bead down to the center of the loom work. In the appropriate location, work a loop large enough to go around the larger bead or button. Run through the row bead and the beads of the clasp several times until it's secure.

MANDALA EDGING

1 Starting at the first diamond point, you will work a short, two-legged Mandala edging at the diamond point and stitch. (Refer to the basic bead weaving instructions on page 19 if needed.) Repeat the combination for the Mandala edging around the bracelet, working from point to point along the diamond motif of loom work. Continue with the three-bead picots along the solid color section.

2 Finish the bracelet with a Mandala edging around the whole rim.

3 Close the edging by stringing one bead of color 1 and running down through the very first bead of the Mandala edging. Run through the nearest row to bring the needle out on the opposite side.

4 Repeat the edging on the opposite side of the bracelet.

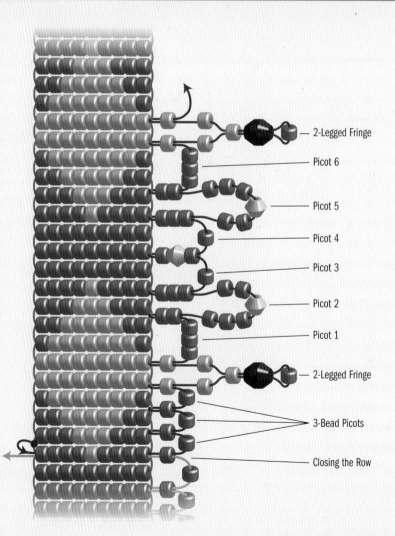

- 2-Legged Fringe
- Picot 6
- Picot 5
- Picot 4
- Picot 3
- Picot 2
- Picot 1
- 2-Legged Fringe
- 3-Bead Picots
- Closing the Row

Contributing Designers

Ana A. Araujo is a creative arts designer, television personality, author, and craft instructor. You can contact her via email at araujocentral@aol.com.

Jill Atkins of Reno, Nevada, began design school at the age of 47 and never looked back. Since that time, she has had two pieces in the permanent collection of the White House in Washington, D.C., is a published author, and an award-winning artist. Her designs are a favorite of the rich and famous and can be seen at www.jillatkinsdesigns.com.

Bethany Barry has been working with beads for 30-plus years, and loves sharing her enthusiasm and knowledge with others, through her books, classes and new store, "Vermont Beads and Fibers," located in Middlebury, Vermont. She has authored a book, *Bead Crochet*. She also teaches classes at her store, as well as nationally and internationally. For more information, visit Bethany's websites: www.beadsandfibers.com and www.bethanybarry.com.

Sharon Bateman is an author best known for her book *Findings and Finishings*, as well as articles in *Beadwork*, and appearances on DIY's *Jewelry Making*. She invented and manufactures the Sharondipity Tube Looms. She is also the author of

The Morning Rose Rosette, Peepers and Creepers, and *Over the Edge*. Sharon can be reached at sharon@sharonbateman.com.

Shari Bonnin is a self-taught jewelry designer and bead artist. Shari sells her jewelry and accessories line, Bonnin Designs, to boutiques and galleries and on her website (www.bonnindesigns.com). Shari can be reached at 714-308-1632 or by email at bonnindesigns@yahoo.com.

B. Christine Brashers began working with polymer clay in 1990, after seeing some polymer beads at a small craft show. She can be reached by email at chrissyfri@aol.com, or online at www.JewelryToMakeYouSmile.com.

Lily Chin is the author of several knitting and crochet books, including *Knit & Crochet with Beads* (Interweave 2004) and *The Urban Knitter* (Berkley 2002). She has appeared on *The Late Show with David Letterman* and in the *New York Times* and *Time* magazine. Lily has her own line of yarns and patterns available at yarn shops across North America. View her designs online at www.lilychinsignaturecollection.com.

Sheilah Cleary is an international bead instructor who regularly teaches in Korea, Singapore, Australia, and all across the

United States. She is a frequent contributor to *Beadwork* magazine and a featured presenter at the Bead & Button Show. Her book *Beading from Beginner to Beyond* has become a best seller. Additional information may be found online at www.SheBeads.com or contact Sheilah directly at shebeads@aol.com.

Doris Coghill left the corporate world five years ago to pursue beading full time. She now spends her time designing kits, teaching nationally, and acting as a show promoter for the Twin Cities Bead Bazaar. Her work can be found online at www.beadsbydee.com.

Kathy Davis brings a unique expression to her work, whether it's art, clay, silver or hand-sculpted polymer dolls. She has been a working artist for over 20 years and has taught for nearly 15. Kathy can be reached by email at davisnet@earthlink.net.

Michele DeFay has been a sewer and knitter in her past lives, and is now conquering the world of beading. Her projects feature Blue Moon Beads, available at www.bluemoonbeads.com.

Jeannine Denholm, an Emmy Award-winning producer, discovered her passion for creating jewelry from vintage beads while scouring Southern California flea markets. Her website, www.Labijoubelle.com, features unique, vintage-inspired designs.

Chris Franchetti is a handcrafted jewelry artisan, writer, and business owner in Seattle, Washington. More information about Chris is available on her jewelry websites, www.chetti.com and www.chettibeads.com.

Beki Haley has been beading for most of her life. Her business of selling beads and jewelry supplies has been going strong since 1985. For more information, visit Beki's website, www.whimbeads.com.

Gary Helwig was working as a telecommunications engineer when his mother, Marge, showed him her handmade wire jewelry. Together, Gary and Marge developed the WigJig family of jewelry making tools. Gary is now responsible for the 1,800-plus page WigJig website (www.wigjig.com), which provides free designs, tips and instructions on making jewelry with wire and beads. Gary may be contacted at gary@wigjig.com.

Judy Hendrix has been a teacher most of her adult life in whatever the current craft. She is a member of the Great Lakes Beadworkers Guild and has appeared on the *Carol Duvall Show, DIY Jewelry*, and seven shows of the new PBS series, *Beads, Baubles & Jewels*. Publications include *Belle*

Armoire, Needlepoint Now, and *Beadwork* magazine in a Fire Mountain Gems advertisement. She can be reached by email at jhen@comcast.net.

Steven James operates Macaroni & Glitter in San Francisco, California. In addition to making appearances on HGTV and DIY, his published work regularly appears in publications around the country. Steven can be reached by email at steven-james@macaroniandglitter.com or through his website, www.macaroniandglitter.com.

Marilyn Johnson has been designing and teaching jewelry making for about twelve years, mostly in the Los Angeles area. She started as a self-taught hobbyist. She wore her own jewelry, which was noticed and which appeared on television shows and music videos. Now she's a bicoastal teacher and knotting guru.

Gail-Ann Krieger, a native-Texan, studied art history and foreign cultures at Barnard College while shopping at every store she could find in NYC. After combing Manhattan for ten years and a stint as an assistant buyer at Bloomingdale's in search of the perfect accessory, she launched Girls Against Boredom, incorporating her studies and style savvy. Contact her online at www.GirlsAgainstBoredom.com.

Nancy Kugel has often been inspired by her trips throughout the United States, Canada, the islands of the Caribbean, and Europe. For more information, visit Nancy's website, www.engee-kay.com.

Akiko Masuda is an Ikebana (flower arranging) master from Japan. Samples of her work can be viewed at her website at www.akikomasudadesign.com.

Cathi Milligan is a California-based glass and jewelry artist. She teaches throughout Southern California and sells her beads and jewelry through her website, www.beadbrains.com, in stores, and at shows. Her work has appeared in *In Style, Bead & Button*, and even a couple of Japanese fashion magazines, and on The Learning Channel, The Lifetime Network and DIY Network. She's currently involved in a project for the Pasadena Museum of Art. She can be reached by email at beadbrains@sbcglobal.net.

Anne Mitchell started her creative career over 20 years ago as a professional lighting designer. Anne is now a full-time designer, teacher, and author. Anne can be reached by email at anne@anne-mitchell.net. View her designs online at her website, www.anne-mitchell.net.